IS IT HOT IN HERE?
(OR AM I SUFFERING FOR ALL ETERNITY FOR THE SINS I COMMITTED ON EARTH?)

IS IT HOT IN HERE?
(OR AM I SUFFERING FOR ALL ETERNITY FOR THE SINS I COMMITTED ON EARTH?)

ZACH ZIMMERMAN

CHRONICLE BOOKS
SAN FRANCISCO

Library of Congress Cataloging-in-Publication Data available.

ISBN 978-1-7972-1757-4

Manufactured in China.

Design by Michael Morris.

The following pieces began their lives elsewhere in different forms. Grateful acknowledgment is made to *The New Yorker*: "The Seven Days of Creation under Capitalism," "First Lines of Rejected 'Modern Love' Essays," and "Consider the Red Lobster"; *The Huffington Post*: "Too Much Cheese"; *Welcome to Kweendom*: "Drag Reveals"; and *Popula*: "Salad."

These essays are works of nonfiction, but some names have been changed so people don't sue.

10 9 8 7 6 5 4 3 2

Chronicle books and gifts are available at special quantity discounts to corporations, professional associations, literacy programs, and other organizations. For details and discount information, please contact our premiums department at corporatesales@chroniclebooks.com or at 1-800-759-0190.

Chronicle Books LLC
680 Second Street
San Francisco, California 94107
www.chroniclebooks.com

To the red-hot sinners,
burning at a heat others can't stand
(who happen to have
seventeen dollars of disposable income)

CONTENTS

SALAD

The battle began at the Myrtle Beach Costco. I was steering a shopping cart with enough food to stock a doomsday bunker when I spotted a bulky bag of spinach.

"We could make a salad," I suggested.

"You can make a salad," Mom answered. "I'm not gonna have any salad."

First blood had been drawn.

Mom's dinner table had always been a parade of simple southern recipes, dishes that seem to say, "We're all gonna die of heart attacks, so let's do it *as a family*." For a newly minted New York City slicker to return home and suggest a salad not of the macaroni persuasion, on Thanksgiving of all days, was blasphemy against God. Of course, I no longer believe in God.

It had already been a challenge for Mom to get me home for Thanksgiving. I'd skipped the last four years, opting for romantic trips abroad with my boyfriend. Now, newly brokenhearted,

I decided to pull a prodigal child: do the right thing and return home.

"Spirit flies direct from New York," Mom texted me.

Going home feels like going backward, I thought but didn't say.

The flight was turbulent enough to induce labor, but we managed to land without any change to the number of souls on board. My entire family—two sisters, brother, Mom, Dad, and my older sister's three children—were in the airport lobby with a "Welcome Home, Zach" sign. The spectacle suggested I was returning from war; I'd just forsaken my familial obligations. My mom smiled and gave me a one-handed hug, the other hand gripping my six-year-old niece's baby doll.

I tossed my tiny bag in Dad's truck and rode shotgun. We talked about the weather and city living. Meanwhile, I worried that if I mentioned my ex-boyfriend too loudly, he might drive us into a ditch. There's a tension in southern air—the strange bedfellows of homophobia and humidity, and the ever-present terror that the person you were might be long behind you, but they are still breathing down your neck.

On Thanksgiving morning, Mom was in the kitchen preparing cardiovascular warfare. I observed her at work with enough distance to be curious, almost ethnographic, and offered commentary on my findings.

"You put sugar in the deviled eggs?!"

"Just a little," she said. Matter-of-fact.

"You know there's already sugar in practically everything?" I explained. "Big Food adds sugar to keep us addicted."

"Oh, is that so," she said, stirring and not changing a thing.

I carved out a corner on the counter and started to put together my simple salad. Spinach, a few tomatoes, some cheese. I'd never really been in the kitchen much as a kid. Chores were gendered and uneven in our house: Women did the cooking, washed the dishes, cleaned the bathroom, kitchen, and living room, and ironed clothes. Men mowed the lawn. On the TV was the Macy's Parade, a fabulous Broadway musical number snuck in between the masculine Spider-Man and bro-y Hulk balloons. I watched it as I finished my three-ingredient masterpiece and asked Mom if I should put on the dressing now or later.

"Yeah, put it on there," she answered. "And stick it in the fridge so it stays cold."

Maybe Mom was warming up to a collaborator in her kitchen, her queer kid doing her work. She told me she loves me, something she says so often it's like she's trying to convince us both.

"Think you'll have any?" I asked.

"Nah, I'm not gonna have any salad."

My two nieces set the dining room table, used so infrequently that it feels like playing house. Every seat would be full this holiday thanks to my older sister's addiction to having children. My nephew and nieces, referred to as "the babies," don't know me well at all, a casualty of my not visiting. A friend told me you can show up for a niece or nephew at any age, but I feel bad that we're not closer.

I didn't grow up in this house, so it always feels a bit fake to think of it as "home." My parents moved from Roanoke, Virginia, to Myrtle Beach, South Carolina, during my first year of college. Generations had lived in a small circle in the Shenandoah Valley, until my entrepreneurial, adventurous mother set her sights on the shore. She built her dream (twenty-minutes-from-the-) beach house.

Her act of generational, geographic rebellion must have been genetic. I was living my dream too, in New York. Ever since high school, when a coach bus drove me and forty classmates to watch the witches of Oz from the nosebleeds, I knew I wanted to live there. After a too-long tour of duty in Chicago, a cataclysmic breakup finally jettisoned me to the city of 4 a.m. bars. I was living my (sharing-a-single-bathroom-with-three-other-adult-humans) dream. If everything turned out exactly as we planned, we'd be very bored gods.

When the meal was ready, everyone took their seats. Dad emerged from hibernation. He looked gentler now than I remembered, a soft, gray beard hiding his neck. He never hit us, except with zingers and Bible verses. A pastor in his past life, Dad could deliver full-length sermons at the dinner table, hellfire and brimstone as appetizer and aperitif to any meal. Today, hunger bested the Holy Spirit.

"Dear Heavenly Father, we thank you for the meal. In Jesus's precious name we pray, amen."

The prayer ended, and my ten-year-old nephew outed me.

"Zach's eyes weren't closed!"

Mom shot me a stare but broke it quickly. A four-year time-out had put everyone on their best behavior. We silently agreed to try to keep things light on Turkey Day. Instead of yelling about atheism, Christianity, Trump, abortion, homosexuality, kids in cages, racism, capitalism, and socialism, we passed the mac 'n' cheese and potatoes.

"None for Zach. Zach's a vegetarian," my younger sister said when the turkey made its rounds.

Our plates were filled and emptied.

"Why don't we all say something we're thankful for?" my mom pitched.

It's a tradition we'd done as children. I always sat anxiously during the game, shame and fear pulsing through my body because I knew there was only one right answer.

"Jesus Christ," my youngest niece said dutifully.

I wondered if her answer would change over time—and as drastically as I had—from a straight, meat-eating, Christian conservative to a queer, vegetarian, atheist socialist. Would she get the space and time to dig and grow, or just pour some more sugar in the deviled eggs?

After a couple more thankful answers—a few Jesuses and a gas price joke from Dad—I became brave enough to share my truth.

"I'm thankful for Lady Gaga."

"Zachary," my mom chided.

I smiled and course-corrected: "I'm thankful to be with my family."

"Aww," she cooed.

Slices of her no-bake cheesecake and a pecan pie from Cracker Barrel, recruited in recent years to help out as the matriarch aged, were distributed. A plastic pitcher of sweet tea met its demise. Dad retreated to the recliner in his bedroom to watch football with my brother, while my sisters cleared the table and loaded the dishwasher. At fifteen minutes total, the meal was more of a feeding than a sit-down dinner. Its brevity kept us from hurting each other. Family members always have the nuclear codes for each other, the precise collection of words and phrases that, when entered, cause total annihilation. Tonight's short summit staved off mutually assured destruction.

I helped my sisters put the leftovers in the fridge when I saw the carnage. Drowning in buttermilk, waterboarded by ranch, wrinkled beyond recognition: my salad. I reached for the bowl to see if any of it could be salvaged, a mother not ready to say goodbye to her child, but the ingredients had already decomposed. I considered taking a bite, but dessert had left me no room.

This victory would go to my mother. Her subtle but effective smear campaign against something green on her dinner table was a success. Perhaps it was a fool's battle to begin with—to push against the juggernauts, the parade balloons of Tradition and Mom and Home—but I tried and failed with pride.

Mom passed behind me as I poured the aftermath into the trash.

"Oh no," she said. "Guess none of us are having salad."

MATCHMAKER, MATCHMAKER

My first kiss was a stage kiss. I'm not sure if it should count. In the second act of *The Music Man Jr.*, Marian the Librarian lays a kiss on Charlie Cowell, anvil salesman, that causes him to miss his train so he can't tattle on the titular musically illiterate conman. When the time came to kiss in rehearsal, I wasn't ready to surrender my virgin lips. With some Scotch Tape backstage, I added a layer of protection.

My first and only successful three-way was at a summer stock theater company in New Hampshire. It was also something of a performance. The building that housed the theater used to be a barn, and the house where the actors lived felt like one. Bunk beds in common spaces allowed thirty people to fit in a house meant for six people who like each other. It also afforded me the opportunity to double the number of penises I'd seen to date.

I was visiting a friend who'd taken on the more-than-full-time job of managing an ensemble of actors. When I arrived, the artistic director asked me to help with the next production, and I responded with the enthusiasm that comes with not having a choice. I was, after all, getting free board for a month.

I'd never operated lights for a show before, preferring to be in the spotlight rather than behind it. The only way I survived thirty back-to-back performances of *Fiddler on the Roof* was by pretending that I was God. The lead, Tevye, delivered his prayers to the Almighty into my spotlight each night, so I convinced myself he was talking to me, for I was Him.

"Without tradition," Tevye said to me, "our lives would be as shaky as . . . as . . . as a fiddler on the roof!"

The Fiddler was a cute boy with thin lips and brown hair. I followed him eagerly with the spotlight, purely for professional purposes. I wasn't out yet, to myself or others. "Homosexuality is a sin" was such a common refrain under my parents' roof that it could have been a song. Turning it down to hear my quiet desires was taking some time. When I asked around about the Fiddler, I learned devastating news: He was dating Motel. Motel had black hair, a ballerina's body, and an annoying laugh. They'd fallen for each other earlier in the season, raptured in the double ecstasy of first love and summer love. I thought this ruined my own chances for summer lovin'; instead, my target expanded.

"How funny would it be," I said to them in the cast kitchen one night, "if we like . . . you know . . . you know. Right? Right?" On my last night in New Hampshire, filled with the confidence of two raspberry Smirnoffs, I made a more articulate, formal offer.

"So boys . . . are we doing this?"

They exchanged a silent glance and smiled.

*

I pressed my prepubescent ear against my parents' bedroom door like a spy.

"Mom! Dad! What are you doing? I need you!" Some dispute with my neme-sister required immediate parental intervention.

"I'll be right out," my mom called back. "I'm trying on bathing suits."

It was December.

She emerged a few minutes later, with a light blue bathrobe and red cheeks. "What did y'all need?"

My parents have never discussed sex with me, but I've come to conclude that the dead bolt on their door on Sunday nights was not for weekly fashion shows.

After school most days, I had the house to myself from 2:30 to 3:30 p.m. I turned up MTV in the living room as loud as it would go and snuck into my older sister's room to smell her scented candles. My parents' bedroom was off-limits.

One afternoon I was working on my display board for the seventh-grade science fair, and I needed a pair of scissors to perform some necessary paper surgery. Judges would assess "The Effect of Light Intensity on Plant Growth" solely on its contribution to botanical science, but it couldn't hurt if the display board was pretty.

I checked the junk drawer. *Nothing.*

I checked under the kitchen sink where my dad's tool belt was. *Nada.*

The utensil drawer sometimes had a pair, but *not today.*

I checked my older sister's room, my other sister's room, then my brother's. The only place left, down the hallway, the Holy of Holies, was my parents' bedroom.

The wooden vanity next to their waterbed was full of stuff: Mother's lotion, jewelry, a poem, but *no scissors.* I decided to check out the ledge at the top of the mirror and climbed up. Above, there were even more odds and ends: a Smucker's jar of spare change, some office supplies, disposable cameras no one had developed. Then my fingers hit a heart-shaped wicker basket in the farthest corner. I pulled it down and examined its contents.

I'd seen a condom once before. In my middle school's library, when I went to check out a book on close-up magic, an unused Trojan fell out. I immediately turned it over to the principal. I would have encountered them earlier, in fifth-grade Family Planning, but my mom reviewed the curriculum and had me removed when condoms were discussed.

In this basket were more condoms than I'd ever seen. Something was under them, though. I moved them aside like dirt in an archaeological dig to reveal a sloppy stack of gray pamphlets, like thin playscripts. The cursive title of the top one danced across the cover: *69 Ways to Spice Up Your Sex Life.*

I closed my eyes for a moment.

Disgust.

Shame.

Guilt.

My chance.

I spread the pamphlets out like flashcards. This was my opportunity to learn the secrets that had been kept from me. The pamphlets were sealed in perforated envelopes like paychecks, so I found one with its edges already torn.

"For Her Eyes Only," the cover warned. I hesitated, opened it, and read the page.

Spice #57: Shaving Your Pussy.

I have collected a handful of regrets in my life—not calling my late grandmother more often, not going to my friend's dad's funeral, and not wearing my retainer at night—but a Top 5 thing

I wish hadn't happened is reading the word *pussy* on a sex pamphlet in my parents' bedroom. At the time, my qualms were limited, though, for I did not yet know exactly what a pussy was. *Vagina, urethra,* and *fallopian tubes* were terms I knew from sex ed, but nary a pussy had I encountered to date.

First things first. If you have never been shaved before, you are in for a real treat. The shave itself is very erotic, and the end result is a beautiful, fully exposed pussy and all its external parts.

The pussy possessed both an inner and outer life. It sounded powerful.

Take a warm shower first. Lay down on the bed or the floor so that you and your partner are comfortable. Relax and spread your legs as far apart as you can.

A real team effort, this pussy-shaving.

Massage in some good-quality moisturizing cream.

I registered my mother's Bath & Body Works lotion on the wooden dresser.

Before you begin shaving, you may want to trim any dense hair with a pair of scissors.

The scissors!

Take special care to shave every inch—the feel of a bare pussy is wonderful.

The last page had illustrations of the various shaves—a triangle, a landing patch, a "blank canvas"—but still no real confirmation of what, where, and why the pussy was.

I was reaching for a second helping of pamphlet when I heard the front door open. In one virtuosic movement, the scripts were back in the basket, covered in condoms, back up on the dresser, and I was kneeling in the living room with my science fair display board, undone.

"Mom," I exhaled, covering my need to catch my breath. "Do

you know where some scissors are?"

"Did you check the junk drawer?" she asked.

"Yeah."

Then she seemed to remember. She opened her bedroom door and came back with a sharp pair.

*

The Fiddler locked the door and lit scented candles. Motel opened his Mac, put on a playlist, and took off his clothes. The mood and music felt like what a thirteen-year-old boy imagined sex to be based on gawdy, over-the-top 1970s porn.

"Why are you laughing?" Motel asked me.

I could feel the Fiddler and Motel become aware of my discomfort and their shame echoing back.

"This is just so wild," I covered.

I knew I needed to embrace the fantasy if I was to get through this without scaring off the actors.

This is a type of performance, Zach. You're a character. Yes. You're not inexperienced, Zach. You are a sex god.

Sex God spoke only with his body and knew every trick to please every partner. He had fucked for millennia, pleasing millions across the globe since the dawn of time. He actually created time just to keep track of how long he could have sex. He lifted his matches with grace and struck them with the fiery passion of the sun to set them ablaze. In his spare time, he also authored a series of sex pamphlets that spice up the sex lives of humans, and led to moderately attended book tours in third-tier metropolises.

When the show was over, I conspired with the Fiddler to meet in the bathroom to continue our fun. Instead, our Smirnoffs did us in and the communal bathroom was used only for its intended purposes.

I spent the rest of that summer under my parents' roof, not forging any new traditions. My parents have a framed poem in their bedroom, propped against a dresser where a wicker basket full of scripts hides. It reads:

In homes where Christ is first
It's obvious to see
Those unions really work
For a marriage takes three.

TOO MUCH CHEESE

As a longtime fan of the Papa Johns brand and its garlic sauce product, I was excited to join the "Better Ingredients, Better Pizza" family. I filled out a short application and was hired with desperate speed. Target, my first part-time employer, required a drug test and an eighty-question "retail associate selector" that asked trick questions about stealing pens. All the Papa needed was a Social Security number and weekend availability.

The first sign that I might not be a good fit came on my first Friday.

"How many people are you feeding?" I asked over the phone, reading from the corporate script. As a high school thespian, I wasn't one to deviate from my lines. "Awesome! Well, we have some great specials for you!"

When I got off the phone, the shift supervisor I'll call Mama John hurried over.

"Just take the order."

"Huh?"

"Just take the order."

"But the little sign says—"

"Don't offer specials."

OK . . .

The second sign that my time with the Papa might be limited happened on the assembly line. In the fast-and-loose world of pizza, cheese is the most prized and expensive ingredient. Dough costs nothing, sauce is really just red water, and toppings are mere suggestion (a lover's whisper of pepperoni, the illusion of a green pepper, an olive sliced so thin it's a memory). But cheese costs cold, hard, shredded cash. According to the corporate Post-it notes above the ingredients, each pizza, no matter the size, gets only one scoop of cheese. I knew better. I knew what the people deserved. Their hard-earned $10.99 plus tax plus delivery fee and tip demanded more. I looked at the naked pizza before me, barely dusted with cheese, and snuck on an extra scoop.

Mama John lunged from the other side of the restaurant and slapped my wrist.

"Too much cheese!" she screeched.

"But it's barely covered."

"Too much cheese," she repeated, taking the scooper from me. "Go make boxes."

I took my lashing and accepted my fate.

In Pizza, drivers are on top, followed by dough-tossers and then the lowly phone-order-takers. Beneath everyone are box-makers. For hours, I was banished to assemble small, medium, large, and (extra-difficult) extra-large boxes. I stacked what must have been a decade's worth of boxes in every corner of the store, enough to give even M.C. Escher vertigo. The work was mind-numbing, but I took my punishment.

The unsung Robin Hood of Papa Johns, taking cheese from the rich to give to the cheese-poor.

What ended my tenure with the Papa wasn't being a cheese martyr but being an artist. When I checked the next week's schedule on the manager's office window, I saw I had been scheduled for Saturday night. Saturday is a big night in Pizza because it's when a lot of people give up. It is also a big night in Theatre. The high school play opened that Saturday.

I went to Mama John at the dough counter to break the bad news.

"Hi there. I was scheduled for Saturday, but I can't do that shift unfortunately. I'm in a new play at school."

I thought I'd be rescheduled, offered a way to trade the shift, perhaps commended on my commitment to the arts. Instead:

"If you can't come in Saturday, don't bother coming in again."

My pizza career ended as swiftly as it began. No goodbye happy hour, no "Good luck on opening night," no "For he's a jolly good fellow" sung charmingly off-rhythm. My calling to make families of four aware of the latest pizza specials and to bring *substantial* amounts of cheese to people who lived too far to order Domino's was over.

I kept my uniform out of spite (I'd paid fifteen dollars for it) before throwing it out a few weeks later.

I could say being fired from Papa Johns was yet another instance of a young artist's dreams being threatened by capitalism, another episode in the overworking and overscheduling of employees in a system that puts people over profits, money over meaning, and the mass accumulation of wealth over the living of life—but that, my pizza lovers, would be too much cheese.

THE SEVEN DAYS OF CREATION UNDER CAPITALISM

DAY ONE

In the beginning, God created the heavens and the earth.

And God said, "Let there be light," and there was light, and it was good.

Then God's boss asked Him to stay late and make the sky too.

And God stayed late to create the sky, ignoring the sounds of the janitor's vacuum. He created it, and it was good.

DAY TWO

On the second day of creation, before God clocked in, God's boss told Him the light that He had created was good, but not great.

"And I took a peek at Your Plan, and I think You can speed it up, God. I'd like to see You create water, land, herbs, and trees today. And a better light."

And God said, "That is a lot, but sure."

And God's boss said, "You're a total rock star, and also God."

So God quickly created water, land, herbs, trees, and a better light, and God's boss said, "Let there be a smile too."

DAY THREE

On the third day, God's boss explained that He would actually need to finish all of creation that day.

When God questioned the feasibility of that, His boss said, "I'm sorry, but on which day did You create all these excuses?"

So God said, "Let the waters bring forth abundantly every moving creature that hath life, great whales, and great—"

And God's boss said, "You can just say 'fish.'"

"Fish," God repeated. Then He said, "Let every living winged fowl that may fly in the—"

"'Birds' is good," interrupted His boss.

"Birds," God said. "I suppose I'll get rid of all creativity and just call them 'beasts of the land,' huh?"

And God's boss asked, "Do You have a minute?"

God's boss took God aside and put Him on a performance-improvement plan for His attitude.

God went back to work, late into the night, and made His favorite part of creation: humans. God saw that the humans were good, and He gave them dominion over all of creation. Then He fell asleep at His desk and the motion-sensor lights turned off.

DAY FOUR

On the fourth day, God's boss woke Him up.

"Why did You give free products to the humans?"

"Products?"

"Everything You create on the clock, God, is a product owned by Heaven, LLC."

"But I created the clock."

"And we're grateful for that. Listen, I have another update: We have to create another earth today. And by We, I do mean You."

"What?"

"Our angel investors need to see that we have an efficient, replicable production process."

So God sighed and said, "Let there be a second light, and a second sky, and a second land." He created it all again, late into the early morning, even though He had tickets to see *Hadestown* with some friends.

DAY FIVE

On the fifth day, God was promoted to Senior God.

"Senior God?"

"Yes! And Senior Gods get to create twenty-five earths per day!"

"More earths? Is that needed—or even possible?"

"With You, God, all things are possible."

God exhaled and got to work. He created a third earth, a fourth earth, and a fifth and a sixth earth. He texted His friend to ask if she could water His plants.

And then God had an idea. He said, "Let there be five tape recorders!" With them, He recorded the instructions for creation, and He pressed play on the tape recorders to create the necessary number of earths.

And God looked upon the earths, and they were bad, but at least there were twenty-five of them.

DAY SIX

On the sixth day, God's boss told Him that He was a genius and that He'd be making twenty-five tape recorders that day.

"But I like making earths."

"You're still making earths, kind of!"

"And these earths aren't My best work."

"Even better! We can sell upgrades. It's all part of God's new plan: Planned Obsolescence."

And God said that He didn't know if He wanted to do this.

And God's boss called Him a Negative Nancy, which kind of hurt His feelings.

So God buried His emotions in His work and created twenty-five tape recorders. And they were bad, and God didn't feel good.

DAY SEVEN

On the seventh day, God called in sick. Then He got an email with no subject line and the message, "Do You have a minute?" So God took some DayQuil and went to work.

There, a great earth-manufacturing plant had been built. Inside, a chorus of thirty dead-eyed angels were seated before thirty OK tape recorders, pressing buttons that said FISH and BIRDS and BEASTS OF LAND.

God wept for His angels being exploited—even some cherubs who were only a thousand years old. Then He looked down at His first earth for the first time in a long time and stormed into His boss's office.

"What happened to the first humans?!"

"It's actually a really funny story." God's boss explained that the first earth was too close to all the tape recorders, so the sound pollution caused the humans to go mad and eat one another.

And God said, "What?!"

"I know, it's very sad, but it is only one earth's worth of humans. We've made thousands of others to date! A small sacrifice. And You love sacrifices!"

God left His boss's office and set forth to create a new plan.

God said, "Let there be a world where labor is not alienated, and labor value is not exploited. Let there be cooperation instead of never-ending, destructive, accelerated competition. Let the needs of My dear, sweet humans be at its center, not the rapid accumulation of profit. And let there be leisure and joy so that life can no longer be so heavy. Let there be, well, light!"

None of that happened. God's creation powers had been rescinded, and the seventh day of creation was His last day.

"But . . . but . . . I've worked here since 'in the beginning'!"

"And we're grateful for that. Gabriel and Michael will escort You out."

"Don't you know who I am? I am the great 'I am'! I am irreplaceable!"

"OK, but You're not Beyoncé. And we found a cheaper replacement."

As God was escorted out, He looked upon His replacement.

Jesus said to God, "Father, please forgive Me." And God called His Son a scab.

And God was dragged out of the factory and cast into the Lake of Fired.

DAY ONE

On the first day of unemployment, God rested.

He created the first résumé, ordered Chinese food, and set up a Google alert for "entry-level jobs but also I'm God."

God thought about His creations and how bad they were, and He wondered if He should've never taken a job at Heaven. His food arrived, and He tipped the delivery angel.

And God ate the Chinese food, and it was very good.

THE TWINK ON THE FIRE ESCAPE

To survive your second Chicago winter, you need a few things: wool socks, long johns, a winter coat, a scarf, gloves, boots, and no memory of your first Chicago winter. I wrapped myself in everything and ice-skated along the sidewalk to meet my friend for brunch.

"There's a thirty-minute wait," she told me. Were the diner's infamous boxing-glove-size cinnamon rolls worth it to Halcyon and me?

They're so good, I said via the silent psychic communication that develops between lifelong friends.

They're not that good, she countered.

"It's BYOB," I said for real.

"We have no B."

"I'll go get us champagne?"

"Deal."

I made the trek to the 7-Eleven across the block to fulfill my promise. I pray my days of gas station champagne are behind me, but the past so rarely stays in the past and God doesn't answer my prayers.

I returned just in time for the host to call my name. He had a pen behind his ear and a smile so perfect that I was sure he never needed braces.

Halc and I enjoyed our meal, DIY mimosas were made, and the cinnamon rolls nearly knocked us out. After they met their fate, my sights shifted to a different sweet.

"The host is cute," I remarked.

"You should give him your number," Halc nudged.

When our separate checks arrived (we were still too young in wealth and etiquette to be treating each other), I went to the restroom to make space for a final mimosa of confidence. I'd never given my number to a stranger, but maybe today was the day.

I tore off the bottom of the receipt, wrote my number, and hid it in my palm like a magic trick. The exit was tight, the restaurant busy, and the host's back to me. I planned to hand it to him and say, "Call me." Instead, I blurted out: "Call me . . . if you . . . want to . . . This is . . . my number if you . . . want it . . ." in self-doubt Morse code. Maybe she's born with it, maybe it's a lack of confidence.

"How'd it go?" Halc asked.

"We have to leave." I grabbed her arm, and we walked back to our apartment.

I assumed I'd never hear from the cute host, but at the top of the stairs to our apartment, I got a text with a perfect smile.

"Hi :)"

*

The twink was sipping a latte, reading a trashy paperback, and eating candied almonds from a Ziploc bag when I arrived for our first date. Outside food was not allowed at the coffee shop. I'd landed a bad boy.

Raised by Disney and parents who will never divorce, I tend to arrive to first dates with an engagement ring; so the early warning signs about him went unnoticed.

"I just moved here!" "I'm nineteen!" "I don't have any friends!" "I call my mom every day!" "I played a lot of hooky in high school."

Red flags look like confetti when you're falling for someone.

For our second date, I brought over a pizza from a new restaurant where you paid extra for the task of cooking it yourself. It has since gone bankrupt. The twink chose our feature presentation.

"You've never seen *Cabaret*?!" he asked in shock.

"I have never seen *Cabaret*."

I was his senior by a few years, but he had been out longer. We watched Liza in his mostly unfurnished one-bedroom apartment while he provided director's commentary. It felt like he had prepared a queer syllabus.

Queer 101

Date #1: *Identify Zach's cultural blind spots, Twink to kiss Zach*

Date #2: *A film screening of* Cabaret; *while Sally Bowles and Cliff Bradshaw kiss on-screen, Zach and Twink do so on Twink's couch; Madonna playlist and dancing until a neighbor asks us to keep it down*

Date #3: *A viewing of* Liza with a "Z," *white wine, sex*

On our third date, the twink went to refill his glass with wine I'd brought over. My eyes began to wander around his home when I spotted his open day planner. On that night, my name was written, which made me smile. But on Saturday, with hearts drawn all around it, was the name of another: George.

I should have taken the disparity in the number of hearts drawn around our names (five against a clean zero) as a hint to dial things down. Instead, this threat to my One True Love story created a sense of purpose and urgency. The student became the teacher as I prepared our next lesson.

Date #4: *Zach takes Twink to a 4 a.m. bar that might not card*

Clark Dog, a hot dog restaurant with a dive bar attached like a skin tag, is known for its pickleback shots, cheap hot dogs, and lax bartenders. When the bouncer accepted the twink's fake, I was delighted to show off that I knew the ins and outs of our shared city. *Take that, George!*

The twink ordered a martini, and I ordered a beer. The twink ordered a second martini, and I opted for a second beer. The twink ordered two picklebacks and put another dollar in the jukebox. It was Tuesday, but when you're nineteen in a bar, it's always Saturday.

"I think I'm gonna call it a night," I announced, hoping he would join me.

"I'm gonna stay out for a while," he responded.

I took the hint, walked home alone, and decided to stop texting the twink.

*

I woke up to pee around 2 a.m. and glanced at my phone. Four voice mails.

"Zaaaaaaach. Hymn clock tout icon ghetty miami mint."

I spoke some Drunk but had never studied this dialect.

"Pees lemmings U2 apart mint."

I called him.

"Zaaaaaaach, aym lahcked hout."

"What?"

"Haim looked pout."

"I'm sorry . . . ?"

"I'mlockedout," he managed.

"Oh no. Where are your keys?"

"Eye uno."

"What?"

"High. Ooo. Knot. O."

This boy was not my problem, but my evangelical upbringing makes me feel guilty when I don't hold open a door. I took him to the bar that didn't card, so this was partially my cross to bear.

"LOT MAY HEN!" the twink screamed at his apartment building.

"You can sleep at my place if you want," I offered.

"What?"

"You can sleep at my place. I can send you the address."

"Wearer hugh? LOT MAY HEN NAY BORES!"

I wanted to tell him to call George for help; instead, I did what I thought was right.

"Hold on. I'll come get you."

I bundled up in wool socks, long johns, a winter coat, scarf, gloves, and the terrifying image of the twink freezing overnight.

"We're gonna do a round trip if that's OK," I told the cab driver. "My friend has had a little bit too much to drink."

The driver nodded, and when we arrived, my diagnosis was confirmed.

"Hope in pup, Sarah! Lemon hin, Natalia!"

The twink didn't seem to register his best chance at shelter for the night was named Zach. I caught him in the courtyard and tried to guide him back to the cab. Swing dancing with an alligator would have been easier.

The cab driver watched our erratic zigzag. In a radical act of compassion, he drove away. On the thirty-minute trek home, cabs avoided us like I was carrying a bucket of vomit with holes in it (and in a way, I was). A cop car added a new terror. I felt like I had a "He's only nineteen, and I helped him get booze!" tattoo on my forehead. We finally reached my apartment and climbed enough stairs to make a cross-country runner feel like a chain-smoker.

"Iafukajsnfewaknfenef!"

"Keep it down. I have roommates."

The twink collapsed on my couch, and I tossed him sheets and a pillow. I was relieved the harrowing late-night adventure was over. We would call a locksmith in the morning, and maybe this guy would fall back in love with me, the person who saved his life.

But this is not the story of "The Twink on the Couch."

When the twink ran to the bathroom, I assumed he was bringing back up his picklebacks. Instead, I heard the shower start.

Please, yes, take a shower in the middle of the night. Do you need any specialty hygiene products during your stay at Chez Zach? Happy to arrange a late checkout as well.

After ten minutes of shower sounds, my anger at his entitlement turned to worry, and I decided to give the door a gentle knock.

"Michael?"

Nothing.

"Michael? Michael!"

My knocks got louder.

"You okay in there, Michael?"

A lifeguard once told me you can drown in just six inches of water, so I turned the doorknob. The door had been locked.

My commotion woke Halcyon, who came out of her bedroom and looked at me, confused.

"Michael locked himself in the bathroom and isn't responding," I blurted out.

Her eyes widened.

My first attempts to break open the door wouldn't have opened an automatic one. Eventually, the fear that I was overreacting gave way to the horror that I was underreacting, and I used the full force of my body to smash the door open.

"Michael?! Michael?!" I screamed as I rushed toward the shower like the killer in *Psycho*. Behind the curtain, all I found was a puddle of water and floating bottles of shampoo. The small window in the shower that we had never opened more than an inch or so to let steam out was wide open. The twink was gone.

I waded through the sea of bottles to look out the open window. Down below, but not quite on the ground, I could see the whites of the twink's eyes looking up.

"Get back up here right now!" I yelled down. "Climb back up this instant!" The twink didn't respond, and the white balls disappeared. I looked back at Halcyon and asked with my eyes, *Do I have to . . . ?*

I think you have to.

I pulled myself through the window like an action hero in an air duct. Outside, I positioned my bare feet on the toothpick-thin rungs of the fire escape. It had started to snow, and like every party I've ever been to, I was underdressed. Gravity and wind from Lake Michigan worked together to encourage me downward.

Twenty terrifying feet later, I reached the twink and learned why he had stopped. The final length of the fire escape ladder, which would allow you to safely reach the ground, was conveniently missing. Directly below was a dark pit of trash bags, which I assumed were filled with razor blades and newly sharpened swords. Beyond the pit, architected by Satan & Sons, was a 10-foot-tall wooden fence blocking it in. The only way out was back up.

"Ike aunt bee leave this."

"We need to get back inside."

"Hut am ide oo-ing?"

The twink started to cry. I hugged him, less out of empathy and more to ensure a large sob didn't accidentally launch him into the chasm below. I catastrophized the headlines: "Area Resident Kills Underage Twink," or if they wanted the SEO bump, "Recent Princeton Grad Kills Underage Twink." I wondered if they would write about me in the alumni magazine.

"How's it going down there?" Halcyon shouted.

"I don't think we can get back up!" I hollered back.

Behind us was a window to a downstairs neighbor's apartment.

"Can you get them to open this window?" I asked.

Really? she eyed.

Yes, really.

Halcyon left to knock on a stranger's door at 3 a.m. In a radical act of neighborliness, they ignored her.

"Taiwan mime tom," the twink whimpered in my arms.

"What?"

"I want my mom," he managed.

I started to rub his back as his words became more understandable.

"I should've never moved here," he concluded.

He was dealing with new city demons, ones I'd only recently asked to quiet down. I held him. I decided to stay by his side until the sun came up or he sobered up. But then, without warning, his crying softened, and a wave of sadness seemed to crash. He spoke clearly:

"Just let me go. It'll be easier."

Legend blames Mrs. O'Leary's cow for kicking over a lantern that set the city of Chicago on fire in 1871, but the city was a matchstick: buildings and streets made of wood, an unseasonable drought, high winds from Lake Michigan that funneled the flames from the Loop to Armitage. Perhaps most tragic was the role human error played: When they first got the alarm, the Chicago Fire Department went to the wrong address.

The fire trucks had no trouble finding the alley behind our apartment. At my high-pitched request, Halcyon had called 911, and within minutes, a fire truck, an ambulance, and a police cruiser arrived. A fireman used a large axe to chop down the wooden fence, climbed over the treacherous garbage, and hoisted a 25-foot ladder against the building to meet us.

"You can climb down, or I can carry you," he offered. I chose to preserve my dignity and climbed down. The twink, who'd left his at Clark Dog, was carried.

Whatever relief I felt when the twink reached the ground was quickly overtaken by terror. Construction bills? Medical bills? Misdemeanor charges? The paramedics began their comprehensive medical evaluation:

"So . . . like . . . what happened?"

Well, there was a very cute boy working at this restaurant that has huge cinnamon rolls. But long story short, he has a date with George on Saturday! Can you believe that?

Instead, we were silent.

"We're gonna have to take you to the hospital if you don't explain what happened," the paramedic pressed.

Suddenly sober, the twink spoke a line that sounded rehearsed:

"I just had a rough night."

"Well," the paramedic replied, "we've all had those." The EMT asked if he had a place to stay and I said yes. With two officers of the law nearby, I was trying to speed up our arrival at said place.

Safe in our apartment, the twink cried some more on the couch before falling asleep. Halcyon went back to bed as well, but I stayed in the living room, one eye trained on the twink until morning came.

My other roommate, Jacob, who'd somehow slept the night through, found the twink in the kitchen the next morning chugging water on the floor. The twink looked up at him and raised his chin: "Sup?"

Jacob helped me repair the bathroom door later that day, and I watched and wondered if the fence outside would be replaced and if I'd be billed. Hours later, I received a text from the twink.

"I'm so embarrassed about last night. That was a really bad night and I really appreciate you helping me :)."

He didn't apologize, so I didn't forgive, one of the perks of no longer being a Christian. I thought about ignoring him, scolding him, or demanding an apology. Another part of me, the worst in me, still wanted to save our love story.

The reply that went through too many drafts read, "That was a really terrible night. We're very lucky that didn't end much worse."

It was my last text with the twink on the fire escape, the boy whose smile caught my eye and taught me a lesson I pray I never have to learn again: You can't force your fairy tale.

SOME FIRST-DATE RED FLAGS
TO WATCH OUT FOR

⚑ He asks the server to repeat the specials but does not order any of them.

⚑ He cites *The Joe Rogan Experience* a nonzero number of times.

⚑ He tries to explain cryptocurrency to you, and when you ask about its environmental impact, he concludes, "You just don't get Bitcoin."

⚑ He refers to his mother as "Mommy" and calls her every day.

⚑ He refers to his mother as "Mother" and never calls her.

⚑ When you ask if he had any nicknames growing up, he says, "Call me Legion, for we are many."

⚑ He says he has a dog, but later tells you he has three dogs, and when you confront him, he says, "It's complicated."

⚑ He says he works in "tech," and when you ask him to be more specific, he states he "creates unique and innovative ways to torture humans for the sins they commit on Earth."

⚑ He orders his steak raw and cooks it tableside with a fireball he creates from his fingertips.

- He asks to compliment the chef and then murders everyone at the restaurant by summoning a horde of demons from the underworld.

- When you ask, "Are you Satan?! Masquerading as a human?! Answer me!" he replies, "Mayyyyyyyyyyybe" and winks.

- He pays the check, but when you get home, you receive a Venmo request for half.

TESTIMONY

In second grade, a nice lady came to our classroom every month to ask if anyone would like to accept Jesus Christ into their heart. No one ever raised their hand—until one girl did. She was taken into a small room, the door was shut, and she came back twenty minutes later with puffy, red cheeks and a certificate that looked freshly ironed.

Despite being on a blue-collar budget, my parents insisted on sending us to a private, evangelical Christian school. There, the word of God was taught every day, and girls could wear pants on Fridays. No prom, no cheerleading, and instead of history class, we had Bible. Punishments were severe. If a student was found to have watched an R-rated movie, they were expelled. An administrator once ordered takeout from Hooters. She is no longer with the school.

By fifth grade, the checkbook didn't check out, so my siblings and I were sent into the den of iniquity: public school.

Surrounded by sinners, I sampled the secular tastes of the flesh: MTV, *TRL*, Barenaked Ladies, The Offspring, *NSYNC, Backstreet Boys. I memorized their songs, sang them back, and even staged a choreographed number with two friends for the talent show. Secular music was evil (music must honor the Lord), but I loved it because it distracted me from my dark, shameful truth: I was going to Hell.

"If you're not saved, Zachary, you go to Hell when you die," my dad preached regularly at the dinner table. "The Bible says in Hell, there is weeping and gnashing of teeth."

He gritted his crooked teeth and acted out a small scream of pain.

"I got saved when I was thirteen, when Jesus came into my heart. I was at Bible camp, listening to the preacher, and I felt something. It was like a presence. It said, 'Jesus. Jesus. You need this. You need this.' And I felt this weight on me, pressing down. It was the Holy Spirit. It kept chanting. So I said, 'OK, God.' And I started crying. I went forward and I prayed the Sinner's Prayer, and I became a Christian."

Dad was trying to save my soul and rehearse his sermon. He made his living as a mechanic, but on Sunday nights at First Baptist Church, he was an assistant pastor. His crowds were never more than forty, but he brought enough fire and brimstone to convert Madison Square Garden.

I sat at the dinner table, terrified. Pulses of anxiety froze me in place like the damning hits of a judge's gavel. What should have been the most comfortable place on Earth (at home with a McDonald's french fry in my mouth) was a portal to Hell.

After dinner, I went to my room and distracted myself with math homework. These questions had answers. I could get them right. I loved the transaction and binary of schoolwork: right/wrong answers that led to good/bad grades.

But eternity, God, and salvation weren't a math problem; they were an essay, and I didn't know the words or the right spell to unlock the answer. I had prayed the Sinner's Prayer so many times that its words ran together like crowded teeth:

*DearHeavenlyFatherIknowI'masinnerandthewages
ofsinisdeath.IknowyousentyouronlybegottenSonJesus
todieonthecrossandonthethirddayHeroseagain.IfI
believeinHim,I'llhaveeverlastinglife.IacceptJesus
ChristasmypersonalLordandSavior.InJesus'sprecious
nameIpray.Amen.*

I prayed in churches, in bed, in school, in the car, and in the shower.

But God never responded.

In sci-fi movies, when there's an explosion in space too loud to be represented, the soundtrack goes silent. It's what God's silence felt like.

I tried everything I could to be saved. I concluded that my attachment to earthly possessions was what was damning me to Hell. At ten, I opened my prized, sealed collection of McDonald's Teenie Beanie Babies and prayed. At thirteen, I tossed my tubes of Proactiv into the trash can and prayed again. When God didn't answer, I retrieved them. If I was going to Hell, I might as well have clear skin.

In high school history, we had to keep a journal like Leonardo da Vinci. In one entry I drew a globe with the eyes of God above it, casting sinning souls into the Lake of Fire. Above the graphic scene, I wrote a verse from the Bible:

"Depart from me; I never knew you."

*

It wasn't until my friend died in college that I stopped believing in God. Turns out the secret to salvation from Hell is to stop believing in it.

My dad emailed me just after I graduated, asking for help editing a paper. He'd been inspired by me being the first in our family to graduate from college to finish his bachelor's degree. He signed up for a class at Liberty University, an evangelical university.

PART ONE—Your life before you came to Christ.

Prior to my salvation, (at age fifteen), I had what I would consider a normal childhood: working Ffather, Mmother who stayed home during the day and took care of the housework. (insert third thing to elaborate on this traditional American idea of childhood) I was never drawn too deep into sin at such an early age although with the unfortunate help of a few friends I was clearly not on the right path. (Can you be specific here about what the wrong path is?) Two things were clear in my thinking as an adolescent to me: ("in my thinking as an adolescent" is wordy and unnecessary) one, I had an aversion to evil and was drawn to things that were good, and two, the theory of evolution was the most comical thing I had ever heard. (Describe looking at the stars on Trinkle Avenue and thinking there must be a god. Paint a scene.) I believed in my heart that there indeed was a God who made everything and thus I began my search for him. At this time I had no

~~real since of being a sinner but was well aware~~
~~that I was not perfect.~~

PART TWO—How you came to see your need for Christ.

It was through listening to Billy Graham cru-
sades on television that made me realize my
need ~~of~~ for a savior. I ~~would~~ watched them as a
little boy in my basement and always prayed the
Sinner's Prayer at the end.

PART THREE—Circumstances surrounding your conversion.

Around age 14, I was invited by a neighbor to
attend a revival meeting. As part of a small
crowd that evening, I listened as the preacher
preached (word choice. "preacher preached" is
redundant) on Hell. I believed his message and
went forward to ~~R~~receive Christ as savior. I
prayed the Sinner's Prayer and left the church
that night with no assurance of a relation-
ship with God and I knew something was miss-
ing. The next day, ~~in the neighborhood around~~
~~my friends the~~ a lady in my neighborhood called
on me to verbally acknowledge my receiving
of Christ which I did. (What does this mean?
You were playing ball and she said "Frankie
got saved!" Paint the scene, don't use formal
language to describe a casual thing.) I began
attending church with this nice lady and joined
the youth group. I began dating the ~~P~~pastor's
daughter and joining in on all the activities
of the youth group. That summer we attended

a youth camp in North Carolina. I will never forget what happened one night. The evangelist was preaching especially hard that night. As he preached, the Holy Spirit pricked my heart and showed me I was not saved as I thought and began to draw me out of my seat and down the ~~Isle~~ aisle. I fought this to the point of shaking in the chair I was sitting in. Finally, as the Holy Spirit's conviction became stronger and stronger, I gave up fighting and said in my heart the words, "~~o~~Okay Lord.~~"~~ The Spirit drew me down the aisle and I sat in a steel chair and was born again. Finally, I understood the Bible! I actually met God and knew I was saved.

Some of my red edits look cruel a decade later, perhaps my attempt to draw blood for the pain he had caused. But it was kinder than correcting him:

I was thirteen when my dad died, and instead of processing the trauma in therapy, I let my grief and undiagnosed obsessive mind fixate on Jesus and salvation. It led to an auditory hallucination, which I repeatedly told to my child, subsequently causing irredeemable doubt, fear, and terror in their life.

That's how I've come to understand what happened. My dad's dad died when he was thirteen, and an absent father sent him searching for a holy one. Granddad's death wasn't entirely unwelcome. An alcoholic who alternated between beating and cheating on his wife caused less harm beneath ground than above it.

"I must have been playing with my food the wrong way one

night 'cause he just punched me across the table," Dad told me. "Nanny slapped him, and we just sat in silence. He never hit me again."

"Did you ever think to tell me you struggled with anxiety?" I texted him recently.

"No."

"Have you ever thought you had OCD?"

"I think I have lived so long the way I am without serious intro-spection and could have a variety of problems."

I couldn't tell if he was making a joke or sharing a devastating truth. Maybe both.

"That and I have grown used to it."

"Have you ever done therapy?"

"No."

"Would you ever want to?"

"Nope."

"I've seen a lot of benefits in my five years."

"I'm sure."

"Understanding cognitive distortions. I'm a catastrophizer."

"Yeah, I do that. Small headache is a brain tumor. Then I work my way back."

My therapist calls it "The Old Place"—where we go when our old, familiar ways of thinking take over. Over the years, I've learned to describe mine: a place of fear, catastrophizing, black-and-white thinking, hypochondria, obsessive thoughts. I've learned that a childhood afraid of an eternity of damnation built pathways in my mind, a decades-long bedrock for anxiety, fear, and shame. It looks a lot like a schematic for Hell.

"Y'all had a good childhood," my mother is quick to say as preamble and postscript to any criticism about my upbringing. From her perspective, we had it made: Our father didn't beat us, we had full bellies, shelter, and new clothes on the first day of school. She and Dad pulled their family lines out of poverty through marriage, hard work, and clipped coupons. Any suggestion that we suffered is not up for discussion.

I've started to call my dad more the further we get from that dinner table on Ichabod Circle. To fill God's silence, we talk. He's started to open up about his father as his years on Earth without him increase.

"He was a sick man," he told me. "I always used to hear my mom say that. I never asked. It didn't seem like something I was supposed to ask about."

Our conversation shifted from his dad to his salvation testimony, a story so familiar I can recite it as well as the Sinner's Prayer. I listen now not out of fear, but courtesy, maybe even compassion, passing secondhand therapy up the family tree.

"It's genetic, this anxiety, this obsessive thinking. I think your dad had it too. He medicated it with alcohol," I concluded.

"You might be right," he agreed.

But I'm not Dad's therapist. I'm his child, and I still want an "I'm sorry." An apology for why I imagine burning in Hell on turbulent flights, after I jerk off, and after naps. For why I have a hole in me so large only Christianity can fill it. For why my journey to find myself has been polluted with the poison of eternal doubt.

"A painful thought I fixated on when I was eight, nine, ten, eleven, twelve"—I listed every age, a flourish he might have used in the pulpit—"sixteen, seventeen, and eighteen was spending an eternity in Hell."

"I told you the truth to keep you from harm," he objected.

"You caused me harm."

"I told you the truth."

EVIDENCE FOR THE EXISTENCE OF GOD

SOME VERY SCARY THINGS

- A friend overplanning a group trip

- Greta Thunberg accessing your Google Flights search history

- A picture of your ex dating a less hot version of you, causing you to question your understanding of your own hotness

- Your unearthed 2016 tweet praising *Hillbilly Elegy*

- Security camera footage showing how much string cheese you consume each night

- A text from your father that says, "Call me"

- Nutrition facts for a cereal you believed to be healthy

- A party where everyone is too young to know who the Backstreet Boys are

- A podcast that lingers too long on a compelling nihilistic point

- The percentage of your life influenced by BuzzFeed quiz results

- The hole in the crotch of your jeans aligning with the hole in the crotch of your underwear, causing what can best be described as a "testicular eclipse"

- Rereading anything you wrote in college

- Your childhood Pokémon card collection bent; your childhood Teenie Beanie Babies collection de-beaned
- Neoliberalism, late-stage capitalism, and nostalgia for artifacts of both
- Pouring your soul into a thing that turns out just OK
- Accidentally replying with the laughing emoji to the sad Instagram story of a near-stranger
- The .000000000000000000001 percent chance anti-vaxxers are right
- A socialist asking how much Marx you've actually read
- Being wrong twice—in a row
- An email with the subject line "(no subject)"

FRENCH KISS

No matter the heartbreaking horrors that await me in my remaining zero to fifty years, no one can take away this: I've had sex in Paris.

I fell in love with John in Chicago, using his bed, body, and cat for warmth during the city's harsh winters. Sweets and sweet nothings are shortcuts to my heart, so when he slipped homemade caramels into my pocket at the downtown Christmas village, I knew he was a keeper. I kept a Google calendar of every date we went on: the first cocktail bar, the first sleepover, the first night at his apartment when I brought Toulouse, his cat, some treats to win over both residents, every play we saw at Steppenwolf and Goodman, our first Valentine's Day at a French restaurant, his homemade heart-shaped cake, celebrating my birthday together with a scrapbook of our love story and a homemade Boston cream pie. At some point I stopped keeping the calendar. It became less clear what counted as a date.

When our second anniversary approached, I surprised John with a cheap flight to the City of Lights. I had made a little mental note that Paris was his favorite city early on, so Paris became my favorite city too. When our office jobs gave us Thanksgiving off, we traded dinner rolls for croissants and heated conversations with family for broken French with strangers.

The turbulent flight ended, and I felt the rush of being abroad and the rush of being. Armed with my extended lease on life, we groggily rolled our carry-ons down cobbled streets to reach our Airbnb.

"I think it's this way." I pointed.

"Are you sure?" John asked. Pointed.

"It's just past *La Place . . . La Place . . . La Place . . . de la . . . République*?" My best high school French accent sounded like I was mocking a people.

At the center of the square was a statue of Marianne, France's Lady Liberty. Normally, she supervises couples dancing to live music until the morning hours; instead, she was surrounded by a fence, flowers, and handwritten manifestos. Two weeks prior, men on motorcycles had opened fire on outdoor cafés and a concert at the Bataclan. John and I had watched in horror from our apartment back in Chicago and debated canceling our trip. It felt wrong to celebrate our love in a city that was in mourning, but also wrong to abandon them. We decided our tourism dollars might be especially appreciated; plus, we both really didn't want to be with our families.

"I am staying *avec ma mère*," our host said as she packed up her last things. She was a university student who'd put her apartment up for rent to make some extra cash. I'd done the same back home, renting out my studio for a week to test-run cohabitating with John before we moved in together.

"Zis is zee bed, and here is zee shower, yes?"

The grand tour took seconds. The shower, a 2-by-2-foot platform wrapped in a curtain, was so small it would've given a flexible magician's assistant trouble. Everything in the apartment had a side hustle: The futon worked the night shift as the bed, and the kitchen sink was pulling a double as the bathroom sink.

We dropped our bags and resisted the siren song of the futon in order to try to adjust our bodies to Paris time. Cheese, bread, and a bottle of wine from a nearby supermarket were our dinner. We fell asleep holding each other while watching Disney's *The Hunchback of Notre Dame*. No one would've mistaken us for locals.

We woke up and made a memory. When I gave John a kiss, we both recoiled. We'd been marinating in day-old American dirt and needed to shower. He went first, and I, left without Wi-Fi, considered the walls. There was a cheesy printed poster that said PARIS, but otherwise they were as bare as the walls of my apartment before I moved in with John. He was a homemaker, so our home together was overflowing with knickknacks, homemade crafts, and sweet decorations to mark every season. I can be sentimental, and I liked John's sentiments.

The shower cut off and John yelped.

"Zach!"

"Yeah, J?"

"Are there towels out there?"

I searched the entire apartment.

"Anything?"

"I'm checking!" John had an Italian temper I wasn't interested in having immigrate to France.

"Well?"

The only thing in the apartment with qualities of absorption was a small, square dish towel. I held it up to my naked, shivering boyfriend.

"You're kidding."

"I'm sorry."

He used the tiny towel, a mop soaking up the ocean.

"Oh, it might be funny now . . . ," he said as he gave me a wet hug.

I put the dirty dish towel on the radiator so it would dry a bit before my go. When I got out of the shower, I dragged the wet, dirty, frigid, damp towel against my cold, wet, naked body. It was unpleasant.

The sights and sounds in Paris distracted me from the pneumonia I was contracting. John had put together an itinerary for me of all the key tourist destinations for a first-timer: *croissants* near the Centre Pompidou, *éclairs* in Le Marais, and *ratatouille* on the Seine. At the end of our first day, we returned to our flat and combined our bodies on the combination futon/bed.

The next morning, we realized we had forgotten to buy towels. We should have run out to buy them immediately. Instead, our eyes panned to the wrinkled blue dish towel on the radiator, arms outstretched like a new acquaintance who is too into hugs.

"Well, we did it once," I suggested.

We took turns taking cold showers and wiping the wet, dirty rag across our bodies. It wasn't any less unpleasant than the day before, but like the second bite of an OK dinner, it was familiar.

Dryish, we ventured back into the city. We ate an *omelette du fromage*, toured Notre Dame, fell deeper in *amour*, and forgot to buy towels. The following day, we went ice-skating along the Champs-Élysées, sipped mulled wine in a Christmas village, ate pricey *petit fours* at Ladurée, and, at the top of the Eiffel Tower, I slipped two macarons in John's pocket. I also made a little mental note of a small bar at the very top where you could buy champagne to celebrate a special occasion.

And forgot to buy towels.

If you had told me at the start of my seven-day trip to Paris that I and another adult human would use a 6-by-6-inch dish towel to take a combined total of fourteen showers, I'd have surrendered our passports at customs. But the decline in dignity was gradual, slippery.

As we left Paris, more in *amour* than when we arrived, we rolled our bags by the statue of Marianne again. A thousand mourners had gathered. A police officer stopped us and searched our luggage. All he found were a few souvenirs and our week-old dirty clothes. We'd done the fine people of Paris a favor and thrown away the dish towel.

*

Our second trip to Paris needed to be perfect. We'd spent most of our third year together apart. I'd gone out to sea to work on a cruise ship and left John for four months at our home. It was a challenge. Our weekly phone calls became difficult to schedule, texts were lost due to poor signal, and we even missed a birthday. There are two competing proverbs about distance: "Absence makes the heart grow fonder" and "Out of sight, out of mind." I didn't know which wisdom applied.

Our trip was once again preceded by tragedy.

"I'm worried," John texted me a few weeks before the 2016 election.

"Spoiler alert: She wins by a landslide," I replied.

When the election returns took a turn that night, we barely spoke. A few weeks earlier, John had gone on a gay bus trip to Iowa to canvass voters that I had skipped. I don't think he wanted to be consoled by me.

A bit ashamed to be Americans, we boarded our Thanksgiving flight two weeks later. The landing didn't bring the usual relief. Everything felt tense: Trump, a terrible flight, and no Wi-Fi. The plane had zero amenities to distract me from the combined terror of fascism and bouncing at 35,000 feet.

The only thing I had control over was helping John find weed. We had two days in Amsterdam before we would board the train to Paris, his—nay, *our*—favorite city, and John wanted to get baked. I get anxious when I'm high, so I was content with a trip of the geographic variety.

Neither of us had made a formal itinerary for this leg of the trip, putting us at particular risk of tourist traps. We roamed unmoored, from country, home, and each other, and took refuge in the land of dildos and old-timey porn. The Museum of Sex, a multistory exhibit devoted to the carnal, took our money and our afternoon.

I wanted to put a bit of thought into where to have dinner, and John seemed to be a bit too high to do much more than eat and laugh. His phone had free international data, so I asked to borrow it. He hid a smile and deleted a text thread.

"What did you just delete?"

"Oh, a text coupon from the pizza place around the block."

We were at the time proud members of our local pizza text coupon club, so his story, on the surface, made sense. But I'm a child of the clearance rack, raised on clipped coupons and buy-one-get-one-frees: I knew the pizza coupons got sent out on Fridays. It was Wednesday.

"Who are you texting?"

He stopped walking and looked at me.

"Maybe we should talk."

We left the museum and found a spot in front of the main train station.

"Do you remember that canvassing trip to Iowa I invited you on?"

I nodded.

"I've been texting a guy I met on it."

I was sitting on a cement cube designed to block someone from driving a bus into the station when my boyfriend drove one through our relationship.

I considered booking a flight to go back home immediately. If I could send a message back through time, I'd tell myself to book it. Instead, we cried and stayed. It felt like we were breaking up, but neither of us knew how. We tried performing still being in love.

The next morning, we boarded the train to Paris and revisited the sites, black-and-white ghosts haunting a once colored-in city.

I sought reassurance during the trip—*Were we breaking up? Could we make it work?*—and John gave me enough for the journey to continue. He smiled at me just long enough. He held my hand just long enough.

"I think I'd like to go to Italy next," John said over dinner at a restaurant we'd returned to for the mousse.

"And who will go with you on that?" I asked, offering an easy emotional support layup.

John paused. "I don't know."

I excused myself and cried in the bathroom.

"It's not like we're breaking up right now," John offered later that night in our Airbnb.

"Wait. We're not?"

John nodded no.

I felt silly for crying so much.

We made a memory.

When we boarded our flight home and took our seats in coach—John by the window, me on the aisle—something felt different. I cracked a few jokes that didn't make him laugh. He locked his seat belt, put on his headphones, and closed his eyes. An hour in, the silence felt too great to last for seven more. To relieve it, I popped the question:

"Are we gonna break up when we get home?"

John looked in my eyes.

"Probably."

The complimentary paper pillow provided by United Airlines on international, long-haul flights isn't comfortable enough to induce sleep, but it functioned nicely to block John's view of my weeping. I went to the bathroom repeatedly to cry. Every time I returned, I put back on my seat belt. Aviation regulations required me to stay strapped next to the man who was breaking my heart.

If we'd broken up on the ground, I could have saved money on the in-flight Wi-Fi I bought to message all my friends; and the other passengers would have been spared the horror of a sobbing 6-foot-4 baby. But our relationship ended in the sky. I got dumped on a plane.

"Can I keep the apartment?" he asked.

"Why would you want to live there? I don't want to live there."

The answer wouldn't come until all my things were in boxes, and I launched one of those post-breakup appeals for closure that never comes.

"I think I got used to living here without you. When you were on the ship."

"You're taking away my home, my boyfriend, and my cat," I said.

"The cat was always mine."

He paid me back for the vacation, and I moved out within the week. I took everything that was mine, so the walls stayed untouched. I was a seasonal decoration in a home that was never truly ours, just his. On my way out, I threw away the bedsheets. It was petty, but I wish I'd done something pettier.

I wonder how much longer we could have stayed together if John had kept his falling out of love all to himself. We could have made it work for another month, another year. The dirty dish towel was just too small to do what we were asking it to do.

My therapist told me that the sooner I got angry, the easier it would be to heal from the breakup. Anger isn't a go-to emotion of mine, so he got upset on my behalf.

"That asshole," he said. "If he had spent less time cheating and more time canvassing, Hillary might have taken Iowa."

FIRST LINES OF REJECTED "MODERN LOVE" ESSAYS

- My husband and I don't text, we don't talk, we don't live together, I don't know where he lives (I have my guesses), and we've never been more in love.

- The vows wrote themselves, pouring from my ballpoint pen like milk being poured from a gallon of milk.

- At the top of Machu Picchu, as the woman I would one day call my wife vomited up the engagement ring I'd hidden in her Nalgene, I caught a glimpse of God's plan.

- I asked Sally to watch *When Harry Met Sally* with me on our third date. My name isn't Harry—it's Henry—but it would have been very cool if it were Harry.

- It felt right when I swiped right, but when he left, I wished that I had swiped in the other direction (left).

- The charcuterie board was covered with meats, cheeses, and a dog-eared letter from my late great-grandfather.

- First, he stole my identity. Then he stole my heart.

- In this "Modern Love" essay, I will argue that although my ex cheated on me with my best friend, I share blame for the demise of our relationship insofar as I could not successfully articulate my emotional wants, needs, and feelings in a concise, productive way during the relationship.

- When I met Sally, I asked if she'd seen *When Harry Met Sally*. She had. I hadn't. My name is Brian.

- "What is love? Baby, don't hurt me," Haddaway sang over the hospital loudspeakers as a baby named Haddaway hurt me during a scheduled C-section.

- I'm Christian. My husband is Jewish. We're getting a Buddhist divorce.

- Of all the Etsy shops in all the towns in all the world, she bought used baby shoes from mine.

- I called No. 54 at the DMV where I work. The next day, No. 54 called my number.

- Men always ask me to watch *When Harry Met Sally* because my name is Sally, but they're never named Harry.

- My wedding day was picture-perfect—it's how I knew that something was horribly wrong.

- Love is like a box of chocolates, in that I like both of those things.

- In rural Alabama, where coyotes holler and jug bands play, "I love you's" are rarer than routine medical care.

- The dick pic looked familiar, as if I'd seen it in a dream; then it dawned on me: it was a picture of my own penis.

- When you realize you don't want to spend the rest of your life with somebody, you want the rest of your life to start as soon as possible. Sally!

- No matter the heartbreaking horrors that await me in my remaining zero to fifty years, no one can take away this: I've had sex in Paris.

SOME THINGS THAT ARE HARD TO FIND

```
A  B  A  D  C  U  P  O  F  C  O  F  F  E  E  R  Y  H  S  Q
G  T  Y  O  U  R  W  A  Y  O  U  T  O  F  A  C  O  N  V  O
D  H  Q  P  F  K  Q  I  X  K  K  S  Z  H  S  G  U  Q  P  F
G  E  A  F  H  E  P  X  S  E  S  O  I  N  Y  S  R  U  C  P
P  R  I  N  C  E  S  S  D  I  B  E  A  N  I  E  B  A  B  Y
F  A  V  T  Q  T  F  W  H  S  X  N  M  A  G  Y  I  D  R  T
Q  P  I  K  H  U  C  C  J  M  C  P  G  P  V  O  R  C  P  Y
S  I  Y  U  P  E  V  I  U  N  J  D  H  M  L  U  T  U  M  O
A  S  N  O  C  A  R  T  F  I  P  X  V  O  B  R  H  R  Q  U
B  T  O  A  U  U  N  I  R  I  Z  S  G  I  N  K  C  E  S  R
B  I  M  U  G  R  L  T  G  U  V  P  V  A  R  E  E  T  P  S
G  N  F  E  P  E  C  X  S  H  E  L  C  I  F  Y  R  O  N  E
D  N  S  T  Y  H  M  O  N  T  T  L  M  X  B  S  T  T  P  L
U  E  T  V  E  D  S  S  M  S  H  W  O  C  V  Y  I  R  S  F
T  T  S  F  H  Y  R  I  B  M  A  A  O  V  N  K  F  A  O  B
K  W  P  I  O  V  V  L  O  C  U  I  T  R  E  P  I  U  Y  K
G  O  P  O  A  X  R  X  S  V  Z  N  C  F  D  G  C  M  X  W
M  R  F  W  W  O  C  F  K  P  L  M  I  W  I  S  A  A  D  T
F  K  C  Q  D  M  U  J  O  D  O  U  Z  T  U  T  T  H  L  F
B  T  C  T  J  F  T  F  W  S  V  L  V  Y  Y  P  E  H  O  J
```

true love
therapist in network
Princess Di Beanie Baby
pants that fit
a bad cup of coffee
cure to trauma
your birth certificate

yourself
your keys
your community
your way out of a convo
the right words
meaning

DRAG REVEALS

1.

In a dressing room, a shy college first-year tried on a black bra, a black dress, and a red wig. The Walmart attendant looked on in dismay. A few hours later, they entered a college drag competition with too little clothing and too much Everclear. You're never fully dressed without a shot. Inebriated and uninhibited, they took to the runway. They danced in the sacred way known only to a nineteen-year-old Southern Baptist whose body knows its queerness before the mind does. A nipple reveal in the final round clinched the title. I won.

2.

I watched my first episode of *RuPaul's Drag Race* for the same reason anyone does anything they don't want to do: a very cute boy. I had just moved to New York, where drag—and my dodging of it—seemed to matter more. During my first year of college, when my only out gay friend, Jacob, invited me to watch the premiere, I said no. A chance choice gave way to inertia; unchecked inertia became identity. But when the aforementioned Very Cute Boy asked me where I'd be watching the Season 10 premiere, I named the only gay bar I could think of.

Therapy was a Hell's Kitchen gay bar where I once went home with a man who controlled his apartment lighting with his watch. I learned this fun fact when he woke me up at 3 a.m. to kick me out. Therapy is also where I arrived on a cold Thursday night to make good on my claim to the Very Cute Boy.

I quickly learned there'd be no talking during the feature presentation. Chitchat was self-policed by a hundred people trying to hear the show projected onto a small screen. During commercial breaks, the TV audio feed, much to the dismay of advertisers across America, was replaced with a local drag queen's commentary. I couldn't keep up with her references.

On my first date with the Very Cute Boy that weekend, we saw the gay high school rom-com *Love, Simon*. I oversympathized with the villain, who was a high school mascot like I had been. I also made a point of mentioning that I'd seen an episode of Mama Ru's program.

"You've only seen one episode?" he asked.

It turns out that only brushing your teeth the night before a dentist visit is not an effective oral hygiene regimen.

There was no second date.

3.

Alyssa Edwards, a contestant on the fifth season of *Drag Race*, quickly became a fan favorite. The smooth southern talker and trained dancer had a penchant for non sequiturs and a signature "tongue pop." She didn't win the competition, but she won the war: a return to an *All Stars* season and a spin-off Netflix series about her dance studio in Texas.

I learned all this in the twenty-four hours before opening for her. In a Google haze, I mined my material for broad appeal gay jokes, penned new drag jokes, and furiously texted my *Drag Race* fan friends for a download on who she was.

I arrived at the venue a half hour before the first show. The cavernous, underground three-hundred-seat theater just off Broadway in Times Square hosted headliners. Tonight would be Alyssa's stand-up debut. *Would she make a reference I wouldn't get? Should I lie and say I'm a lifelong fan?* I was terrified I was going to be fired but also convinced we were going to become best friends.

I walked through the kitchen, feeling at home with the servers, before knocking on the closed dressing room door. A beautiful southern belle (from the waist up) greeted me.

"Hi, I'm Zach, your opener."

"Oh, hi, Zach." Alyssa was mid–costume change. We stood in awkward silence.

"Is there anything you want me to say?" I asked.

"You can say you've seen *Alyssa's Secret*, and now it's time to see Alyssa."

"Alyssa's what?

"*Secret.* My web series."

My research had not covered the web series.

"Of course. Yes."

I said thank you and closed the door. I wasn't sure if I'd been made.

The venue started to fill up with gay men, straight women, and their very supportive husbands. I started to worry I'd be outed as a *Drag Race* denier introducing a god I didn't worship.

I took the stage, did my set, and said Alyssa's name a lot (the trick to opening for anyone). Your main job when opening for someone is to not be that someone, and I was very good at not being Alyssa Edwards. When my ten minutes ended, I introduced a video. When her prerecorded voice gave way to her live one, the audience responded in a way I'll be jealous of until the day I die.

"Hello, Caroline's!"

Alyssa appeared from backstage in high blond hair and a long fur robe. The audience sprang to their feet and clapped and hollered. The slower she walked, the wilder they became.

"I thought I was on Broadway. They got me in a diner!" she joked. The audience died.

I stood in the back corner with the bouncer, having lost my seat to a paying customer, and understood nothing Alyssa said for an hour. All I understood was that she was killing. I witnessed the rapture of gay religion, the lightness where we all seem to become one just above our heads, but I was an outsider to her cult.

Before the final show, Alyssa's assistant came over to me.

"Alyssa wants you to wear this." He handed me a blue 8-foot boa.

The blue, queer snake around my neck resurrected my knowledge of good and evil. I took the stage with a new, queer energy, my hips unlocked, my arms freed from my sides.

"When Alyssa Edwards asks you to wear a boa, you wear the boa," I told the audience. They applauded in agreement.

After the show, I snuck back to the dressing room.

"Where we going out tonight?!"

"Oh, baby, I got a 6 a.m. flight. I have a dance class to teach tomorrow."

I went and bought a round of shots and snuck back into the dressing room. Alyssa's things were being thrown into suitcases by two assistants.

"Shots! Shots! Shots!"

"Oh, I don't drink, baby."

"Oh."

An assistant felt bad and did one of the shots with me.

"How do you come down after a show like this?" I asked.

"Oh, I take a long bath. I've got this down to a science."

I started to leave and saw the assistant to the booker. I was tipsy enough to ask, "How did I get this gig exactly?"

"We wanted someone gay," she said, "not too fabulous."

4.

"Are you coming to Bushwig?"

All year, a friend had hyped an upcoming drag fest to me as an accepting, queer utopia. I bought my ticket and saved the date.

Unsure what to wear, I donned a black mesh tank and a haphazard collection of ropes ("Random rope play is not safe," a festivalgoer reprimanded me) and put some of my friend's makeup on ("You look like that meme of the young girl with bad eye shadow and bad lipstick," a friend pointed out).

At the festival, drag divas and pop princesses served genderbends and death drops, constructions and destructions, presentations and provocations, with tucks and twists and boobs and butt pads and smoky eyes—all for wrinkled dollar bills and the screams of their people.

After a few numbers and enough Vodka Red Bulls to feel like college, I heard the audience erupt in a familiar way. Nina West, recently baptized into RuPaul's TV empire, took the stage. The festival was mostly edgy local queens, but no one is immune to celebrity. Nina performed a Disney medley with clips from *The Lion King, The Little Mermaid, Beauty and the Beast,* and double *Mulan,* paired with quick-change outfits from each princess. Recognizable chords and color patterns awoke a secular chorus of queers in the Queens warehouse. We had sung these songs in the carpeted living rooms of the '90s when *Love, Simon, Drag,* and *Race* were just nouns. Old was reborn through lip sync and the sacred recitation of secular Bible verses, fringe gospels that forged a new queer canon and community. Culture bound us together so we could lose ourselves for a moment, the queen a lightning rod to help us connect with the clouds.

I was also pretty drunk.

So I started crying.

I cried at the coming together of people who were left out. I cried for the nostalgia I missed out on because of the culture I'd banished. It must be what Jacob and the Very Cute Boy feel when they watch *Drag Race,* what the crowds felt for Alyssa, what the room was feeling for Nina, what I had felt but forgotten as a first-year. I cried because when you grow up feeling on the fringe, it's easy to reject an invitation to come inside.

New nostalgia washed over me like applause, like community, like sweat at the college drag ball when things were ever clear.

THANK YOU FOR YOUR FEEDBACK

Against my will and better judgment, I built an advertising career. College was four years of learning how to swim, only to be thrown out of a plane. So I jumped at the first stable office job that would support my nighttime creative ambitions and slowly climbed the ladder. As a friend explained, "You bloom where you're planted." As I understand it, I find money hard to turn down. By day, I was an overpaid businessperson; by night, an unpaid clown.

I was underqualified for every role, which meant I rose through the ranks quickly. You might think a marketing job requires a certain level of knowledge and pedigree; it's actually quite the opposite. The less you know, the better. The confidence that ignorance allows is unmatched.

When I arrived at the New York office, my manager, Cathy, a chain-smoker from New Jersey who went to Atlantic City for major holidays, welcomed me to Times Square. In my first week,

I saw Chris Hansen on the street filming a segment, Stephen Colbert's studio, and the Broadway theaters I'd idolized as a kid.

Cathy suspected this job was just a job to me, but she was willing to make it as OK as possible to keep me there for as long as possible. She also gave me a warning about my new direct report.

"Peter was fired from his last job, so he's kind of always anxious about being fired. You should say hi."

I had to pretend to like this job enough to convince someone else to also like it. The hardest part about managing other people, I learned, is that you can no longer lie only to yourself.

I went over to Peter's desk to say hi.

"What? Do you think you're better than me?" Peter asked.

"I'm sorry . . . ?"

"Your shirt. It's tucked in."

"Oh," I said. "No. No, I don't think I'm better than you."

It was the beginning of our fruitful collaboration.

My main job responsibility was reminding Peter every day that he wasn't going to be fired. That way, he could get his work done, so he would subsequently not be fired. I needed him to be good at his job because I did not know how to do mine. I constantly reassured him and told him things were good, even when I didn't think they were.

In my defense, what I lacked in technical skill, I made up for in empathy. In my weekly one-on-ones with Peter, we talked less about work and more about life: his mind, his hopes, his love life. Within a month, he'd met a young woman, which gave him a certain pep in his step; within another week, she'd shown him the door, which gave his shoulders a certain sink.

I stepped into action. I may not have known how to do advanced Excel functions, but I knew how to comfort the brokenhearted.

The Times Square Applebee's is the largest Applebee's on Planet Earth. A trio of hosts welcomed us to the megaplex, and another trio of servers brought us oversized burgers that helped Peter swap his heartache for an ache of the stomach variety. I wanted to be the cool boss, a good boss, so we drank a lot of whiskey at 1 p.m. You only get dumped once.

We stumbled back to the office and got nothing done for the rest of the day.

Cathy took me aside.

"Just a heads-up: Janet starts on Monday."

"Who's Janet?"

"My new boss," she told me. "So your new boss."

People are like instruments, and some just don't sound good together. For example, I'm a guitar, and Janet was a bad boss.

It started her first week. I was presenting a meaningless PowerPoint while she was eating a kale salad. Suddenly, she stopped chomping.

"Do you see what's wrong with this slide?"

I wasn't sure.

"There's a typo," she answered.

"Oh."

She paused for her applause break. When it didn't come, she filled the silence.

"Never send decks to clients with typos."

If advertising were my everything, if as a kid I had dreamed of being the chief marketing officer of Taco Bell or Starbucks, of designing ads for billboards rather than hosting *The Tonight Show* and *The Price Is Right* concurrently, I might have taken my lashing. Instead, I said, "Well, now that you've shamed me in front of my colleagues, can we move on?"

She was taken aback. "Oh, I wasn't trying to shame you."

"Oh."

This was the beginning of our fruitful collaboration.

Our next project together was challenging too. When a snowstorm hit the city, I knew this was a chance to minimize my contact with her, so I sent a note that I'd be working from home. She replied instantly:

"There's no snow at the office."

I looked out my window at a snowstorm that had a name.

Our largest clash, though, was when she dragged a project on until it coincided with my college reunion. I had pulled an all-nighter, sent the project out, and felt the rush of being done and the prospect of incoming nostalgia. A friend drove us down the New Jersey Turnpike to the place that changed my life, and I joined my classmates on campus for a weekend of bad beer and good/bad memories. As we toasted the alleged best years of our lives, I got an email.

"Why was this sent to clients without my approval? This is completely unprofessional and inappropriate."

A meeting request appeared on my calendar for Monday.

I pulled a Peter and started to freak out that I was being fired.

Then, I felt disturbed that I cared at all.

When did this survival job become a career? Why had I climbed a corporate ladder without questioning where it went? There was something about being on campus—the place where I first got to explore my identity and passions—that reminded me of who I was. If this sounds like an advertisement for a liberal arts education, recall that I did waste seven years in advertising.

So on the hallowed ground where I got and gave my first blow jobs, where I did improv shows that didn't matter for drunk students who didn't care, I made a decision.

I walked into Janet's office on Monday to announce I was quitting. I pictured my colleagues storming in to applaud the clarity of my vision and crowd-surf me to the lobby. Instead, the half-hour meeting lasted two hours. We replayed every single disagreement we ever had—the typo, the snowstorm, the "unprofessional" email. By the end of it, we'd aired our grievances and built a decent foundation for working together—just in time for it not to matter.

"I realize this is strange timing, but I've made a decision."

Her disappointment that I hadn't said something sooner was overtaken by her joy that the thorn in her side was being removed.

"I'll let the team know."

She didn't try to stop me. Cathy might have. Maybe she would have convinced me to stay for another month or another year. Maybe I'd be the unhappy CMO of Taco Bell with two kids and a very hot husband named Jeremy. But Janet let me go. Janet was a bad boss.

I still text Peter on occasion. He recently applied for a better-paying job and asked me to be a reference. I forwarded him all the questions they emailed me, copied and pasted his answers, and sent them back. He got the job, I heard, and climbed up another rung.

#2

With a graduation rate that teeters around 50 percent, William Fleming High School hosted commencement ceremonies that were true celebrations. Mothers cheered, aunts and uncles screamed, and all were discouraged from bringing air horns into the Roanoke Civic Center.

The "smart kids" were seated onstage, a close-knit group who, except for a random choice between Spanish and French, had shared identical schedules since sixth grade. After templated advice from an (un)motivational speaker, uneven harmonies from the school choir, and rehearsed remarks from the new principal, the salutatorian and valedictorian were invited to speak.

I was no stranger to the stage—I had starring roles as Reverend Shaw in *Footloose* and Don Quixote in *Man of La Mancha* under my belt—but my friend Henh, the salutatorian, was nervous. He had a sharp sense of humor (he made sure I was aware of my fluctuating weight; I called him "#2" and he called me "fatty"), but he didn't excel in front of large crowds. The speech wasn't a competition, but I was going to win.

Henh took the podium and shared his story. His family had immigrated to the United States from China when he was a baby, and he showed up in public school not speaking English. He climbed his way up to be second in his class, working part-time jobs and doing community service.

"To finish the moment," he quoted from an Emerson poem we'd read in English class, "to find the journey's end in every step of the road, to live the greatest number of good hours, is wisdom."

He ended with a reveal: He had just passed his test to become a US citizen. The audience gave him a standing ovation.

My speech was about birdhouses.

Henh won.

*

I was in a college religion class, The Biblical King David, when I saw a news story on my laptop. There'd been a shooting at Virginia Tech. I texted all my friends who went there. All of them got back to me except one.

My mom called me later that day to let me know Henh had died.

In a fugue state, I met with a school administrator who helped me book my first flight.

"We have a budget for these sorts of things," she told me.

I took a walk around the campus at night and found myself at the chapel. I don't know if I was searching for quiet or searching for words. It was late, so the church was empty. No music, no voices, no profound revelations. As silent as an empty classroom.

When we landed in Roanoke, the pilot made an announcement.

"Ladies and gentlemen. We've got a pair of parents of a student at Virginia Tech on board. Out of respect for their loss, we're going to ask you to let them disembark first."

I wanted to stand up and scream, "My friend died there, too! *My* friend died at Virginia Tech!" But it felt like bragging about something I wish weren't true.

My mom and dad picked me up at the airport, and we rode in silence. When we got home, I went straight to bed. My old room had been turned into an office, so I laid in my brother's bed and wept.

The next day, my mom brought me a pill from my dad's new Xanax prescription. I said no. I didn't want to dull any of this pain. The pain was my memory of him.

The next day, she tried to console me. "Henh's in a better place," she said, "if he was saved."

I closed the door.

The following day, our old high school drama teacher, a balding Catholic man who looked like how you might imagine Shakespeare looked, let all Henh's high school friends hole up in a rehearsal room to reflect. Our old French teacher joined us with cassette copies she had made of one of Henh's final French oral exams. He was in a French class when bullets pierced the door. Based on where his body was found, he was helping to barricade the door. A paramedic at the scene said later that she was overwhelmed by the sound of dozens of cell phones ringing.

Henh's family invited me to see the body with them. I'd been given the title of "Henh's best friend," even though I felt we'd grown apart over the past year at different colleges.

When I saw his body, I had the urge to cross myself, and a

thought came to me that didn't feel like my own: "This is why religion exists. To make this hurt less."

I googled "how to write a eulogy" the night before Henh's memorial service. I'd put it off in the hopes that if I didn't write it, his death wouldn't be real. Trying to write a *good* speech to give a *good* performance for a *eulogy* felt fake. The more I thought and wrote, the more the words themselves felt fake in the face of this. I searched the phrase "silence is truth," and the Buddha appeared in Google.

The memorial service was held in the high school theater where I had played Don Quixote and Reverend Shaw. They played a video of Henh's salutatorian speech. What should have been the first of many important speeches was now his only one. At the end of it, he introduces me. I eulogized my friend. I cried a lot. My speech was OK.

At the burial, we threw yen into Henh's grave and burned incense. His gravestone read "Henry"; he'd changed his name when he became a US citizen to lessen the discrimination he faced.

His death was the birth pang that gave way to my change—my questioning of religion, which gave way to questions about sexuality, politics, desire, doubt. Henh is even why I'm vegetarian. A few days after his death, I happened to watch a documentary on factory farming, and the violence made me nauseous.

Henh will never know the person I've become, and I can only guess at who he might have been. He would probably make fun of this essay.

The last time we saw each other was the Thanksgiving of our first year of college. The smart kids met at Applebee's for a mini-reunion, chatting about our new classes, possible majors, living away from home, making new friends. When dinner ended,

Henh and I weren't ready to call it a night, so we rode around in my mom's red truck. With Top 40 on the radio and the windows down, we did laps around the mall where we both held part-time jobs. I don't remember what we talked about.

HOW TO WRITE A EULOGY

SEVEN NEW SINS—AND TORTURES TOO

NEW SINS

- Interrupting a party that is going well to force everyone to play Mafia

- Engaging in bad-faith discourse about topics that do not materially impact your reality

- Suggesting a book club book you've already read

- Telling someone at a party you will send them a poem that completely changed your life, but never sending it

- Sampling three ice creams at the ice cream shop and not ordering any of them

- Breaking my heart

- Using the word *nonzero*

NEW TORTURES

- You are brought to a gorgeous multistory library and told it contains all the wisdom of all time and you can spend eternity receiving all the condensed wisdom of the ages, only to realize slowly that every book in the library is a copy of J. D. Vance's *Hillbilly Elegy*.

- You are given six delicious Cadbury Creme Eggs and told one is filled with mayonnaise. (They are all filled with mayonnaise.)

- Your friends tell you that a new TV show is "amazing" and "incredible" and "cured my depression," but the show is only just OK, causing you to lose all faith in your friends' taste.

- You are followed by a celebrity on Twitter, you tell so many friends about it that it amounts to about 15 percent of your personality, and then you are suddenly and without reason unfollowed by the celebrity.

- Your body is frozen and given to your conservative, evangelical Christian parents, who read Bible verses to you every night, which you can hear but not respond to.

- You are never featured on your barber's Instagram account. (Is this not your best work, Doug?)

- Your ring tone is changed to a reference to a late '90s Budweiser beer commercial: "WASSSSSUP."

CONSIDER THE RED LOBSTER

Mom has been a server at Red Lobster since Reagan served as president. When I was growing up, unclaimed takeout seafood had a habit of showing up in our fridge. You could say I was born with a Cheddar Bay Biscuit in my mouth.

While the Red Lobster menu changes seasonally, rolling out a new script of specials for her to memorize, the wage has remained the same: $2.13 an hour plus tips. Two thirteen is a bad guess for pi and a good time for a nap, but it's not a living wage. It's up to the customers to add a few dollars to the bill for silly things like Mom's mortgage. So she puts on a show for tips and because, as she says, "I do love meeting people."

She collects stories from ocean-bound tourists, Yankees who have moved South, and customers from abroad who occasionally laugh at her joke that "standard tipping in the US is fifty percent." She likes telling her stories too: about her "silver fox" husband, four kids, three grandbabies. If you've had my mom as a waitress, you've definitely heard that I went to Princeton, live up in New York City, and don't call her enough.

One Thanksgiving, I surprised her during her shift. When I came in, a host whom I'd never met hollered, "Zach's here!" She swung by my table later: "We've heard so many stories about you." I watched Mom bounce around her tables and chat with her coworkers, a mother hen to a gaggle of twenty-somethings. She smiled when she saw me in her section, took my order, brought extra ranch, and refused my tip.

At a press conference in April 2020, Henry McMaster, the governor of South Carolina, announced the reopening of the state: "Our goal was to cause the most damage possible to the virus while doing the least possible damage—at least permanent damage—to our businesses." Three days later, he told the accelerateSC task force that "the last thing any of us want is to have a relapse." He might as well have named the task force "toofastSC." The beaches were reopened immediately, followed by hotels and indoor dining. Dine-in restaurants were especially dangerous for spreading the virus. On May 11, they reopened.

Mom wanted to get back to work.

"I'm not gonna die till it's my time," she told me over the phone a few months after everything shut down. "I don't live in fear. I'm not a worrier. I guess that's part of being a Christian."

But God wasn't the only one steering her through the pandemic.

"I think he did a damn good job." *Did*. Like it was over. When I asked her where she'd been getting her news about Trump's handling of the virus—a question we both knew the answer to—she joked, "*The View*." The rest of the call jumped between the personal, the political, and the religious in the frustrating, familiar way our conversations have since American politics, the media, and I changed. She celebrated Trump's travel bans on China and Europe like they were the vaccine and shared her theory that the Democrats were trying to destroy the economy so they could win the 2020 election. Michael Flynn, Twitter censorship, Bill Gates vaccine conspiracy theories—the Fox News talking head on the phone is the woman who shared midnight crab legs with me in the kitchen.

"The Bible says you don't work, you don't eat," she said.

"Who would have ever imagined that we'd be having over a thousand positives every day?" Governor McMaster asked on July 1, during the first press conference in which he wore a mask. "The responsibility lies not with someone stopping you, but on you stopping you."

It's your responsibility, says a parent to kids playing in a sandbox full of razor blades.

After the aggressive reopening of South Carolina, cases in the state skyrocketed, bolstered by an influx of tourists to Myrtle Beach. Spring- and summer-breakers were becoming infected and bringing the virus home. Seventeen high school students in Ohio. A hundred in Washington, DC. When my grandma in Virginia got tested for the coronavirus, the nurse asked if she had visited Myrtle Beach.

My mom, a perpetual people person, struggled during her first shift back.

"It's hard to talk to your tables. I can't talk to them the way I used to. The mask is so hot." She described a hack to me in which she turns her mask upside down so that it's a little easier to breathe. "Things just feel eerie. It don't feel right. Not normal. People weren't as friendly as they normally are."

New procedures were put in place: temperatures taken at the

start of shifts, masks in customer areas, every other table left empty. But the hardest adjustment of all?

"I love babies, and I can't get close to babies. It's terrible!"

Coming from the woman who said she preferred me as a baby, probably because I didn't talk back, I believe her.

"Are customers taking it seriously?"

"Acting like nothing's going on," she answered. "One couple did wear a mask. One guy sanitized the table."

It wasn't until July 3, three months after the first coronavirus death in Myrtle Beach, that the county council voted, 8 to 4, to require masks for customers in indoor businesses. When *Good Morning America* asked Brenda Bethune, the mayor of Myrtle Beach, if the city took any responsibility for spreading infections, she answered, "People spread this virus, not places."

What changed my mom's mind about the dangers of the pandemic wasn't a call from her kid but one from her own mom. Nanny had tested positive for the coronavirus.

"She was taking it so seriously," my mom said. "I'm mad." She caught it at a funeral, for my great uncle Oscar. She was wearing a mask, others weren't.

"Everything was starting to reopen," Nanny told me, through weak breaths on her flip phone. "So we thought it was OK." Her landline kept ringing in the background during the call. "I'm gonna have to get me a telephone operator," she said.

We talked about how she was feeling ("I just need to get my strength back"), politics ("I don't know why these people worship him. . . . He looks like a chicken"), and the virus.

"I don't think it will ever go away."

"It will, Nanny," my older sister promised.

"Not in my lifetime."

My older sister ended the call by asking Nanny if she could

pray for her. I bit my tongue and listened to the prayer.

"Fourteen of your family members have the virus now," my mom tells me.

"Has that changed your opinion of it?"

"It's hitting a little closer to home. It's awful. My momma's done some suffering the past two weeks. It's bizarre how bad it is. The virus spreading and killing people and hurting people."

I wanted to say I told you so, but when that's true you never can. I wanted her to say that she's been failed by her news network, her president, her governor, her mayor, and her employer. I wanted her to say that she's been failed every day with $2.13 an hour and failed again with the accelerated reopening of dining rooms and funeral homes.

Instead, she said she's made a decision.

"I told Red Lobster I wasn't coming back until further notice."

For the first time in my lifetime, Mom's not a waitress—just Mom.

"What are you gonna do?" I asked.

"I guess I'm gonna learn how to wait tables online."

MOVING & STORAGE

My phone is out of storage. It's overwhelmed by photos, videos, voice memos, city sounds, landscapes, memes, people, places, things—nouns, mostly. Deleting files feels like deleting memories, but in actuality most of them hold the emotional significance of a toenail.

When I tried to clear it out, the first item was a ninety-second video from 2017 of the Hollywood Medium, a twink who struggles with eye contact, talking to Alan Thicke. The Medium tells Alan that he has a message from beyond from someone who died of heart trouble, a safe guess when talking about a man. There's a pause, and then Alan says no one in his family has ever had heart problems. It's one of the funniest things I've ever seen. How can I be expected to part ways with this ninety seconds of unbridled joy to make room for photos of my insurance card?

The state of things under my bed is no better. Tetris-stacked boxes filled with odds and ends: a box of college papers where I argued theses I didn't believe, a box of mementos from my relationship with John, even a box of magic tricks. I don't identify as a magician, but a magician once told me, "If they find a box when you die, you're a magician."

I think if all my belongings were suddenly set ablaze I might feel a kind of relief. I've defaulted to keeping everything; but if everything is important, is nothing important?

My first chance to part ways with some of my stuff was after college. Mom arrived at my dorm ready for our double-digit-hour drive home, and I hadn't packed a thing. Tickets from movies became occasions to replay the occasion and plot. Playbills prompted me to listen to the score from that one show one more time. Four years of books and double-spaced pages sent me down memory lane.

"We need to hit the road," my mother said. She looked at my belongings, exhaled, and pointed to two spots on my bed.

"Okay, this is our 'keep' pile, and this is our 'toss' pile."

Textbooks were no longer filled with memories of the heated classroom discussions; they were two tons of matter that needed to be moved. T-shirts that no longer fit, symbols of the years when I tested the limits of my identity and liver, were just T-shirts. Over ninety minutes, four years of transformational change, a cum towel, and an unfortunate piece of rotten fruit were reduced to two piles. The toss pile was exclusively rotten fruit.

My next chance to get rid of some of my belongings was when John got rid of me. Jacob helped me pack, brought over Chinese food, and wrapped my plates and bowls in Chicago's daily paper.

"Which glasses are yours?"

"Well, we got these Christmas mugs together," I explained. "So I guess one is mine and one is his?"

The process of untangling lives proved difficult emotionally and logistically. I cried while trying to determine whose fork was whose.

"What about this?" Jacob asked. It was a macaron-making kit John and I had bought in Paris. We'd never used it.

"Keep."

"Really?"

"I don't know. Maybe I'll become a pastry chef."

The gap between who I am and who I think I might become is never larger than when I'm packing.

*

Liquored up on too many Cosmos, a friend of mine recently lashed out at me for forgetting that he was born in the South.

"You need to remember people's stories, Zach!"

I could tell I had touched an old wound and called him the next day.

"That's a thing for me," he explained. "I'm afraid of being forgotten."

Is that why I keep all this stuff?

I read somewhere that our brains keep the most important facts we need for survival, but our modern world asks harder questions than which color berries are poisonous or which bush that lion was hiding behind. Maybe I think inside one of these boxes is a key to a lock I haven't encountered yet that I'll need to open one day.

The "Memories with John" box is filled with tickets to plays we saw together, photos, a scrapbook he made of our first six months, and playbills. It's a bomb that won't be detonated until I have the armor of a husband and three happy children, so I move it like Sisyphus from apartment to apartment to smaller apartment.

I heard a rumor that someone in my extended family is a hoarder. They just bought a second home, filled with so many things that maintenance workers couldn't reach a leak in the roof. Maybe there's something in my genetic lottery/cesspool that predisposes me to hold on to my belongings like I'm clinging to the edge of the cliff of obscurity.

The biographers of tomorrow will appreciate my comprehensive approach though. The ragtag team of curators, psychologists, authors, and religious leaders assigned to pore over my artifacts will thank me.

Then, in a museum (landfill), patrons of the arts (ants) will observe, consider, and misread my effects.

Or some twink will use them to pretend to summon me long after I've moved on.

NOTHING IS FREE

Some days I feel like an orb of divine, transcendent light that has severed the cord of desire, no longer experiences suffering, and floats above problems like a cherub on a cloud. Other days, I plot the murder of the guy doing construction in the apartment above mine.

An eight-week online meditation course first got me in touch with the former. It was free, one of my favorite four-letter words, and during the lockdown I had nothing to do. It was time to do nothing.

"Let's all take a moment to close our eyes and become aware of our breathing," the instructor began. He was a kind and gentle man, like meditators often are, with a bald head, as the enlightened often have.

"It might have been some time since we checked in with ourselves. So just take this moment to become aware."

Despite the airy nature of his language, the class had been

developed at a medical school. Jon Kabat-Zinn's pitch was that if people with chronic pain could experience pain without judgment, they might suffer less. Contrary to many of my life choices, I am open to suffering less.

Eight other meditators on my screen—some young, some old, some hippies, some businesspeople—closed their eyes. My heart rate sped up. I closed my eyes and welcomed the thoughts of the enlightened:

This is a waste of time. What's the point? My butt hurts.

Over the course of two hours, we did some short guided meditations and light yoga. It was hard, but when the class finally ended, I felt refreshed and renewed. I was even looking forward to the next session a week later until I learned there would be homework: an hour of meditation a day, every day.

I begrudgingly laid on the floor of my apartment the next morning and listened to a recorded guided meditation.

"What does your toe have for you today?"

Frankly, my toe wasn't giving me a lot of data.

"Now focus on your other toes and up your left foot," the recording continued. "And up your left leg."

There was a sensation on my leg at least, which made me wonder if something was wrong.

"Thoughts, emotions, and bodily sensations come and go," the recording seemed to respond. "We are simply observing them without judgment."

But my butt like really hurts. Am I dying? Also, what if a tweet of mine is going viral right now? I should check my phone.

I finished the session, stretched my butt, and checked my device for the waterfall of texts and likes. Nothing.

Every day for the next six, I laid on the floor of my tiny apartment and trained my brain to focus on parts of my body where nothing was happening. At our next group session, everyone shared stories of how hard it was to make time for the assignment. I was unemployed, so time wasn't the problem; it was just spending time alone with myself that scared me.

This is a waste of time. What's the point? You're worthless.

"During our fifth week, we'll be doing a full day of silent meditation," the instructor let us know. "In a way, this is all practice for that."

*

After my first year of college, when I learned not everyone is an evangelical, including myself, I decided to find out as much as I could about "all the other crazy things people believe." A web search of "summer Buddhism," funding from my school's Office of Religious Life, and flights from Virginia to Texas to Tokyo to Taiwan took me out of the country for the first time.

Venerable Yifa, a 5-foot-tall nun with a shaved head, greeted me at the Taipei airport. She was laughing like she knew something I didn't.

"Welcome, Zach! You will enjoy your time here, OK?" she assured me as she guided me toward a white van. For the next thirty days, I would live like a Buddhist monk.

The monastery was a sort of college campus: dorms, a cafeteria, classrooms, gardens, pathways, and a village of meditation halls. Forty other students and I stayed four to a room and were given off-white robes to wear. Days were filled with lectures on classic Buddhist texts, and nights with silent meditation. Less was more here, so nothing was everything: no laptops, no cell phones, no meat, no self.

We used chopsticks—a novelty to me at home, a necessity here—to take our meals in silence in a large dining hall. Our last bit of bok choy was used to mop up any final pieces of rice in our soup bowl. Nothing was wasted. Our minds and our bellies were full.

In the presence of religious authority, I rebelled. When we took brooms to an abandoned part of the facility for "sweeping meditation," I questioned the enlightenment value of the activity. The swarm of mosquitoes we disturbed agreed. Some participants decided to shave their heads as a sign of detachment from desire and freedom from vanity. I opted to keep my locks.

The trip culminated in a weeklong silent meditation retreat. We entered the dimly lit rectangular meditation hall that would be our home away from home for seven silent days. Our seats were around its perimeter, and our eyes were looking downward as even eye contact broke the silence.

Seated meditation is particularly challenging for the tall. I'm mostly leg, so folding my tree trunks up in nice, neat, sturdy ways is a struggle. Enlightenment might be the remit of those already a bit closer to the ground. During the first day I stretched them as far as I could, but the dull pain brought negative thoughts.

What's the point of this? Why am I even here? This is a waste of time.

"Focus on your object of meditation," Yifa instructed.

Frustrated and bored, I decided to sing through *Legally Blonde: The Musical.* One and a half *Legally Blondes* before walking meditation, another Act One before lunch. On the fourth hour of silence on the fourth day, during my ninety-second recitation of Elle Woods's journey of self-actualization, my mood plummeted. I felt separated from my home, friends, and family, from verbal connections, jokes, and conversation. The silence hurt, like someone ignoring your screams. Frustrated, I opened my eyes and saw my peers: forty little unmovable mountains on their mats. I wasn't alone at all.

The week ended in a pilgrimage to the top of a small mountain. We took two steps, then bowed on our knees, rose, two steps, bowed, two steps, bowed. When we reached the top of the summit, a large golden Buddha shrine looked down. I felt awe, not at anything divine, but at the human discipline that built this figure, standing tall 100 feet above us all.

*

When it was time for my one-day digital silent meditation retreat, the instructor covered his clock. The more I had meditated during the course, the more familiar I became with my particular stream of cruelty.

This is a waste of time. Go do something. You're worthless.

I'd listened to these talk tracks for decades, but for the first time, I could feel how they were affecting my body. It took a year of silence for me to hear how the noise of my mind, the stream of negative self-talk and judgment I didn't question, was adding to my suffering.

This is a waste of time is the waste of time.

I placed a hand on my heart, a move the instructor had taught us, and gave myself some love. For lunch, I had some Starbucks brand string cheese. The next day I opened my phone and in the stream of close-up selfies, jokes, status updates, and news—real and fake—I saw a familiar nun in a brown robe. Yifa was livestreaming her meditation.

"The first day, I did the online meditation with no preparation,

OK?" Yifa told me after I messaged her to catch up. "The second day, the camera was sideways. Ninety degrees upside down!" She laughed.

"How many people watched?"

"The first night had six hundred viewers on the Facebook live-stream. The second: twenty viewers."

She laughed again.

"If my purpose is to become a guru with one million people, that life is lousy. I would try to please these people."

Always a good teacher, she turned the conversation toward her student.

"Don't just follow the outside. Zach, if you don't have your own inside life, you will get lost, OK? Our life has up and down, success and failure, perfection and imperfection. *C'est la vie.*"

"Is that a Buddhist teaching?" I joked.

"It is French."

My joke had not landed.

"Buddhism mentions *dukkha*—life is suffering. Not painful, but unsatisfied. When you are not satisfied with your life, you are suffering."

I complained to my landlord about the construction above my apartment, and he offered to lower my rent. With the extra funds I joined a coworking space that boasted a quiet room. On my first day, I took a seat in a cubicle by a few other workers. It felt sacred, silent, like the meditation hall in Taiwan, where little mountains worked on their own and together to not drown in the waterfall.

Just as I got to work, a jackhammer operator got to work outside. The machinery shattered the silence.

I paused, took a deep breath (in and out), and put in headphones.

Murder would just add to the noise.

HOW TO MEDITATE

SOME KEY INSIGHTS FROM MEDITATING

- Donuts are delicious.

- Passwords that auto-populate defeat the purpose of passwords.

- You can learn a lot of valuable life skills by joining a pyramid scheme.

- The best part about being single is the 100 percent certainty I'm not in a dead-end relationship.

- Everything is different. Everything is the same.

- Open relationships are unfair because I cannot compete in the sexual marketplace with people who already have the confidence of being loved.

- We are interconnected enough to cause global pain and suffering but not yet coordinated enough to alleviate it.

- People are rarely the monsters we see in our minds.

- Someone else's lack of empathy is not a defense for yours.

- Our hearts are connected by strings we can't see.

- *Lust* and *slut* are anagrams.

- Everyone is a fourth grader.

- Donuts are delicious.

A NEGATIVE REVIEW OF
MY NEGATIVE SELF-TALK

Zach Zimmerman's debut album, which featured a trio of Billboard-charting singles ("You're Ugly," "You're Not Talented," and the ballad "You're Completely Devoid of Value and Worth"), introduced the world to a young, hip iconoclast. Even the lesser-promoted songs ("You're a Worthless Sack of Shit" and "You're Going to Wear That? In Public?") revealed we were in the presence of a trailblazer.

But if *Negative Self-Talk* spoke to a generation, Zach's sophomore album, *I'm Trying Really Hard to Be Happy Now*, panders to one. Where lyrics once popped with painful truths ("Look beneath the surface / There is no purpose"), now they are cake pops ("I'm putting my baggage up on the shelf / I'm trying really hard to love myself"). Pardon me while I put my vomit in a toilet. The album's singles ("Therapy," "Cry for Help," and "Heal Your Trauma, Momma") are not earworms—they make me wish my ears had been devoured by worms.

My big question (besides "Why, God, why?") is this: Was the first album the fluke, or the second? How can the same mind that created the hits:

- "Hi, My Name Is Garbage"
- "You'll Never Know Love"
- "You're Not Conventionally Attractive"

- "Alone, Alone, Alone, You're So Very Sad and Alone"
- "You're Not Funny, You're Just Tall"

and the bonus *Hypochondria* EP tracks:

- "Am I Having a Heart Attack? (You Are)"
- "I Think I'm Dying (You Are)"
- "Hypochondriacs Always Believe Something Is Wrong with Them, and the Sad Pill Is That They're Right"

also generate this fluff:

- "I'm Trying to Be Gentle with the Idea of Myself"
- "Art Might Be Unhealthy for Me to Make Right Now"
- "While I Rationally Understood My Trauma, I Needed to Feel the Healing in My Body"
- "Have You Read Any Audre Lorde?"

When the album turns meditative with "Cognitive Distortions" and "Lexapro, Wellbutrin & Other Lifesavers," I had to turn it off. Fans will be upset, enemies will be delighted, and The Wiggles will be disappointed to learn they have a new competitor in the saccharine kids' music space.

I won't say Zimmerman is completely devoid of value and worth (we were already warned in the first album); I'll just say that if I were charged with reducing the most human suffering on Earth with a single act, I would develop time travel technology to go back and burn down the recording studio that gave birth to this pathetic, navel-gazing, self-help nonsense of an album. Zimmerman might be "trying really hard to be happy now," but Zach's work makes me, nay us, anything but.

BIRTHDAY SUIT

Birthdays were invented by Big Alcohol to trick extroverted twenty-five-year-olds with disposable income into buying thimbles of well liquor. Like a person who realizes banging their head against a wall weekly might not be in their long-term best interests, I found that binge drinking lost its novelty when I came off my parents' health insurance. With my and Halcyon's thirtieth birthdays on the horizon, we ditched the bars and opted for private, quiet, contemplative self-care.

"So we're naked but there's food?" I asked.

"I guess so? I'm not sure."

The drive was thirty minutes from East Williamsburg, giving us both time to process our nerves and excitement.

"But there's a pool?" I asked.

"There's a pool. And my friend said you can get a scrub."

"What's a scrub?"

"You lay on this bench, and someone washes and scrubs you?"

"Nude?"

"Nude, I think."

"Oh, wow."

We arrived and stepped out of our Lyft and toward the electric doors of the Korean day spa. A many-floored complex, Spa Castle had no royal family; instead, for $40, customers were kings and queens for the day. I felt more jester.

"The locker rooms and clothing-optional areas are downstairs," the man taking our money told us. "Cafeteria up one flight, and all-gender pool on the roof."

He handed us each a uniform: blue for boys, pink for girls. Designed to keep Toms from peeping in the women's area, the shirts had a time travel effect: It's 1950, gender is a binary, and neither of us have been born. We changed into them and headed up two flights of stairs to an outdoor pool. It had different levels and areas with game show–style buzzers to activate pressurized jets under and above the water. We pushed a few buttons, but the pressure was by all accounts lackluster.

"What's The Waterfall?" Halcyon asked as she pressed a button.

Without warning, a Poseidon-level attack was waged from above. A small child would have left this mortal plane, but because I'm large enough to not be swept away, and young enough to have not yet made my great piece of art, I had the strength of body and purpose to remain on Earth a bit longer.

"Should we do the nude areas now?" Halc asked.

Do we have to, I eyed. I've been trained to hate my body by evangelical Christianity and gay culture. Christians taught me that the flesh is sinful, evil, and wicked, and a drag queen at The Box once lifted up my shirt and told the twink I was trying to court that I "have rolls." In the locker room, I removed my clothes and managed to avoid eye contact with a man across the way. I headed into the private pool area wearing nothing but my religion.

It felt odd at first, air and wind hitting areas that are normally protected, but with a dozen or so other nude bodies around me, I acclimated to the new cultural norms. Plunging into the pool felt like putting on clothes, so I dove in. I was covered and warm, and a jet was giving a slight massage to my lower back. After a spell, I opted for the steam room. Then, with a good sweat, I dipped myself in the chilled bath. A few seconds in there sent me back to the warm pool where I began. I started to feel a bit OK being naked.

In the calm, I realized that the guy from the lockers had followed my exact sequence. Was he following me, or was that just the order of things? I also realized he was hot. And short. I'm built like the Leaning Tower of Pisa, so I've always appreciated the structural integrity of the short.

Without pomp, he suddenly joined me in the warm pool. There was a tension in the air—the bedfellows of humidity and homosexuality.

"What's that thing do?" I asked.

"Oh, just squirts lots of jets at you," he responded.

"Oh, nice."

Did his brevity suggest a lack of interest in me or the simplicity of the jet situation?

"It's my first time here," I offered.

"It's my . . . third or fourth time?"

"Oh, nice."

The jets filled the awkward silences. Was every sentence drowning in subtext or was the pool of double meanings drained?

"Where do you live?"

"Allentown, Pennsylvania. You?"

"Williamsburg."

"That's far."

"Well, Williamsburg, Brooklyn."

We concluded our conversation while the jets continued theirs.

We had no clothes to signal sexuality, only our gait, mannerisms, body hair hygiene, and presence of tattoos (we both had none). I got up and went to the sauna.

If you ever doubt that humans can communicate in an invisible way beyond our conscious comprehension, spend an afternoon in a men's steam room. Subtext, among other things, is substantial.

There were a handful of naked men in the sauna when I arrived, cycling in and out based on their tolerance for the heat.

The hot man followed me in.

Slowly, the other men left. When we were finally alone, and the slot machine returned two cherries, the man and I had been in there for quite a while. Our fingers had pruned and sweat mixed with the steam on our bodies. I decided to pop the question.

"Do people . . . masturbate in here?" I was an anthropologist collecting data, detached, a journalist searching for truth.

"Yeah, some people do."

His response still left us stranded in the ocean of possibility. This couldn't be mere coincidence, I decided, as I went from general to specific.

"Would *you* like to masturbate?"

Even the steam vents held their breath. The fit, short man from Allentown, Pennsylvania, answered:

"Well, yeah!"

He shuffled closer to me, giddy.

"We just have to be . . ." and he didn't have time to say "discreet."

We traded looks between each other's religions and the door to make sure no one was coming in. I leaned in for a kiss, which might have been a steam room hookup violation, and he returned it briefly before kissing elsewhere. The fear of being caught added to the eroticism of it all and was just plain terrifying. What interrupted our steamy love affair was capitalism.

"I have a conference call I have to get on," Allentown confessed.

I wasn't ready for the encounter to end, though, as neither of us had quite "pushed The Waterfall button" yet, so I made a modest proposal.

"Want to meet back at 1:30 p.m.?"

"Sure."

On my way to lunch with Halcyon, I made a 2 p.m. appointment for the naked body scrub and fantasized about the level of relief I would soon feel: my nude body being bathed after my rendezvous with Allen. Romance, rest, and relaxation. I might ascend.

After lunch, I returned and joined Allen in a cold pool.

"What do you do?"

"I'm a physical therapist. How about you?"

"I'm a comedian."

"Nice. I have a lot of respect for comedians. I think it takes a lot of vulnerability."

He moved near me and grabbed my thigh. We were sitting too close for anyone to think we were doing anything other than what we were doing. I continued the masquerade of our pleasant, platonic conversation.

"What's Allentown like?"

He stopped, maybe taking my question as asking him to, or maybe multitasking is hard for him. He does tend to focus on one task at a time. That's Allen.

My body scrub appointment interrupted us this time.

"I'll be back in thirty minutes."

When I checked in for my scrub, I learned there'd been a double booking. I'd need to wait an extra thirty minutes. I was frustrated—both logistically and sexually. But this meant more time with my dear, sweet Allen. I returned to the pool to surprise him and was shocked by what I found. Allen with another man.

Well, well, well. What do you have to say for yourself, Allen? Didn't think I'd be home this early, huh? Well, here I am! Here I am asking how are we going to tell our kids their father is a tramp?

I went to the sauna in a huff and grew wistful. There was the bench where Allen first blew me. I barely had time to reminisce before someone sat next to me. It was Allen. But he was not alone.

If Allen thought that I was surrendering our home to some harlot, he had another thing coming.

Is this some game to you? "How many dicks can I suck at Spa Castle?"

The new twink called silent dibs on Allen's dick. I settled for his balls. Frankly, I thought it a bit too early in our relationship to open things up to a third, but that's Allen. He moves fast. Maybe this is what our relationship needed, I thought: a new, shared experience to spice things up.

A stranger opened the sauna door and Allen tried to turn his bent-over sucking into some sort of "oh, it's too hot in here" gesture, which launched him out of the sauna. I was glad he nearly got caught. We'd have to talk about this later. It was time for my scrub.

A man in only shorts stood before a leather table and tapped on it twice. He adjusted my towel to a courtesy position, blocking my salvation from view, and began his process. The sensation of a bucket of warm water being poured over me brought back infant memories that don't live in any conscious, rational place.

The man motioned for me to turn, and I did so. My childhood memories gave way to more recent ones. How Allen and I first saw each other at the lockers. How we talked in the pool together. "What does that thing do?" Such a goofy, nervous first thing to say. We were younger then. Things were easier.

The man exfoliated my back, then scrubbed my butt.

Allen wasn't perfect, though. He put his career ahead of me, cheated, and invited a third without discussing. But I was willing to make this work.

The scrubber had reached my feet when I saw Allen get back into the pool where he first grabbed me under the bubbles. I smiled at him before watching him scoot closer to someone: another other man.

I watched in horror as my body was cleaned while the love of my afternoon betrayed me. My scrub ended just in time for me to see Allen get out of the hot pool and shake the other person's hand like it was a pleasure doing business with him.

Things were over between Allen and me, I decided. I managed to give him a final flash of eye contact so he could sense my judgment. Divorce papers were to be shipped to Allentown.

I toweled off, got dressed, and headed back up to the lobby.

"Relaxing?" Halcyon asked.

"Very."

On the ride home, I brought her up to speed on the sandcastles I'd painted in the sky with a man in the steam room.

"That's kind of far, isn't it? Allentown?" she asked.

I plugged it into the map on my phone.

"Two hours, it looks like."

"I think it's a pretty conservative place too," she commented.

We were quiet the rest of the ride home. Relaxation is exhausting.

The New York City skyline came into view. Home looks most beautiful when you're coming back. A few hours later, a man whose name I'll never know would see the skyline too, on his two-hour drive away from who he is.

CLOTHES ENCOUNTERS

The stakes at the American Eagle could not have been higher. It was the day before the first day of middle school, I needed to fit in, and I did not want to be there.

Mom was thumbing through the clearance rack and threatened to embarrass me if I embarrassed her.

"Don't show your butt," she warned me. "I'll make a scene, too."

She tossed me a pair of marked-down jeans, and I headed to the fitting room.

"How's it coming along in there?" she asked.

I struggled into the jeans, opened the curtain, and walked a catwalk that turned into the Green Mile. Nothing debunks a middle schooler's sense of independence quite like their mother checking how well their pants fit.

"Room to grow, that's good."

The shame in the fitting room was only the beginning. When Mom got to the register, she asked if there were any promotions going on. My head became acquainted with the floor as she announced via megaphone, "We don't belong in this store! We can't afford this merchandise!"

"Do you have a credit card with us?" the cashier asked.

I said a small prayer that God didn't answer.

"I do now!" Mom replied.

The new card's 20 percent off shopping spree was a death sentence to our afternoon. We went back to the rack. If we didn't spend, we were burning money. We left the mall when it closed.

"You know, Mom used to sneak clothes through the window of my room so Dad wouldn't see," my sister told me. "She had me remove all the tags and hide the bags."

Despite disliking their acquisition, I was grateful for new clothes at school. A classmate making fun of your outfit was the end of the world, so armed with new fits and my "outfit calendar," a daily log of which clothes I'd worn in which combinations on which day, I made sure no bully would ever levy the most terrifying accusation: "Didn't you wear that yesterday?"

The outfit apocalypse waited until college.

If I had fully understood the level of wealth I was surrounded by at Princeton, I would have picked wealthier friends—and robbed them. I was on need-based financial aid among a zoo of brand logos (alligators, whales, horses, oh my). After my first year, I returned home and reported to my mother that I needed Ralph Lauren polo shirts.

"Oh really?"

Mr. Lauren wasn't on our approved list of go-tos, so my mother investigated him online. The price tag removed her jaw from its hinge.

"Sixty dollars?!"

Ever the hustler, she searched for a deal. An eBay auction for "10 multicolored RALPH LAUREN POLO SHIRTS!!!" caught her eye. She bid. She won.

"See. There's always a deal."

For $60 plus shipping and handling, we were the proud owners of ten new polo shirts. I folded them in neat rectangles and returned to campus.

Preppy and prepared to be fully accepted by classmates in top tax brackets, I met another fate.

"Is that a fake polo?" my friend Steve asked.

"What?"

"The polo player. He's, like, at an angle."

I looked down at the embroidered gentleman. He was defying a bit more gravity than he should have been.

"Oh my god, Zach. That's a fake polo."

Steve kept his laugh mostly to himself, but it was too late. The scarlet letter had already been branded on me. I felt like an alien whose human flesh suit had eyes where the ears should be. Later that week, a Goodwill in New Jersey became the proud owners of ten new "Ralph Lauren" polo shirts.

"Mom wore her brother's hand-me-downs growing up," my sister told me. "She got picked on bad for it. It's why she wanted us to always look nice."

Since taking on the thankless responsibility of outfitting myself as an adult, I largely subscribe to a "get away with it until someone comments" mentality. I try to put off buying new clothes until my being tattered becomes the talk of the town. When the hole in the crotch of my jeans was no longer visible only to me, I made a trek to the mall.

Uniqlo has a stretchy jean product that has made me a lifelong fan. People think you're a martyr of tortured beauty, suffering in tight jeans, but they couldn't be more comfortable. This store didn't have my size, so I grabbed an aspirational pair from the rack and went to try them on.

Long an adult in the eyes of the law, I still felt a pang of childhood shame and fear in the fitting room. The woman who embarrassed me as a kid was who I needed as an adult. Someone to force me to try on the clothes and tell me how they looked. I needed someone else to inflict the pain to help me grow—the necessary growth in this case being to cease wearing jeans that reveal the blinding paleness of my inner thighs.

The pants did not fit. I asked an employee if he had my size in the back, and he asked if I had tried searching online.

I concluded that the hole in my current jeans wasn't *that* big. I could avoid crossing my legs, take shorter steps in public, and only attend dimly lit functions. Not wanting to leave empty-handed, I did a lap around the clearance endcaps. I'm still an infant when it comes to understanding my own style and taste, but I found two discounted T-shirts that looked cute.

I sat them on the register, and an involuntary impression came out of me.

"You don't have any promotions going on, do you?"

They didn't, but the cashier asked me if I was a student.

"I'm a student . . . of the world."

She charged me full price.

FASHION TRENDS FOR THE END OF DAYS

The future might look grim, but you can still look trim! With Armageddon just around the corner, it's time to get dressed to impress, bitch! Here's what's *in* as we run *out* of livable habitat:

1. Layers, layers, layers! Layers are super helpful when you need to sport several outfits at once, and are also super necessary when responding to 100-degree temperature swings.

2. High-waisted pants are in, guaranteed to show off your gorgeous ankles and help you wade through the high sea levels.

3. Second-skin tops hug you like a warm blanket and reduce your exposure to increased radiation, girlie.

4. Oversized jackets, blazers, and cargo pants might hide your hourglass shape, but they are so in for storing dehydrated food supplies.

5. Belts are back! Define your tight, tiny waist, gorg, and have an on-demand weapon against the alleged zombies (sightings to be confirmed).

FASHION TRENDS FOR THE END OF DAYS (UPDATED)

As the flesh from our bodies is peeled away by radiation poisoning, many are questioning the function of fashion. But just because aliens are snatching our bodies doesn't mean we can't look snatched, babe! Here's what's *in* as we run *out* of time:

6. Chain necklaces draw the eye to your neck and can function as blunt objects in the war against the now-confirmed zombies.
7. Hoodies are an easy way to show off your casual side and afford anonymity during the class war.
8. Full-body jumpsuits are a fun way to spice up your look and are now required when outside the bunker.
9. Camouflage is fun, retro, and disguises you from Peter Thiel's robot dog army.
10. Fanny packs! Hold that bulky walkie-talkie since the cell towers have fallen and carry your government-issued cyanide pill since social order has collapsed, mama!

FASHION TRENDS FOR THE VERY LAST DAY (UPDATED)

On this, the evening of the last day of Earth, we want to thank you for your readership and let everyone know that fashion is a lie. It's been an honor to provide what are useless tips and tricks during the Final Tribulation. Should life begin again, we hope future generations will value comfort over fashion and know that what is *in* is whatever you want to wear *out*. Except fanny packs over the shoulders. We don't deserve to rebuild if we keep doing that, hunty.

RAINBOW BRIDGE

The free version of Grindr has ads that aren't for queer-specific things like circuit parties or TV shows with older white women in emotionally unhinged roles; they're for addictive mobile games. A cartoon fish needs help escaping death or an old man needs to dodge drowning, and you must solve a puzzle to help. I don't engage with mobile ads on principle (the industry took a half-decade of my life; I won't give it any more), but after a particularly lengthy string of app conversations duller than plasticware, I decided to look for fun in one of the games.

After consenting to the presence of in-app purchases, I was the proud owner of a digital aquarium. By completing puzzles, I earned coins that I could use to buy greenery, decorations, and a variety of fish. I vowed to never spend actual money in the game, but the very smart people who designed it swore a competing vow. After an hour of gameplay, I was one move away from the one thousand coins I needed to buy a new clown fish, but I didn't have any moves left. I authorized the $1.99 purchase. To date, I have adopted over seventy digital sea creatures across fourteen aquariums, investing more than the cost of a few romantic Italian dinners.

I was considering adopting a real-life pet when I visited the Brooklyn Cat Cafe with Halcyon. Forty kitty cats roamed free while humans paid a small fee to bother them. Some were sleeping, some jumped around from perches, and others fought for playthings. One cat I gave quite a good pet to had a bit of poop hanging from his tuchus. I left satisfied with the duration of the feline encounter, but months later, in the height of the pandemic, the call of the meow grew.

"Zach, you are a cat," Halcyon told me. "You should absolutely adopt a cat."

I was living by myself, except for a mouse that dropped by erratically and never called ahead.

"Why wouldn't you adopt a cat?" she asked.

I took the nudge and visited the cat cafe's website to explore the application.

Please tell us why you have chosen this particular (set of) cat(s).

The description for Tinkerbell was littered with homosexual dog whistles: "sassy personality," "a fan of cat dancer toys," "her favorite thing in the world is to lay on the bed and soak up the morning sun." I think I could provide a nice, accepting home for a fellow queer in need.

Have you ever had to give up a pet? Why?

We let our childhood dog, Samantha, poop on training pads in the basement bathroom rather than taking her for walks. My sisters and I promised to clean up after each visit, but when my mother checked our work, we were reprimanded and sentenced to clean what became affectionately known as the "poop room." When Mom broke the news that Sammy would be given away, we were a bit relieved.

Have you ever owned a cat before?

Our home remained pet- and poop-free until my sister brought home Ginger. Without warning or discussion, our house was a cat's house. The orange and white furball took an instant liking to me, pressing her head against my chin, occasionally giving it a few licks and a little nibble. Someone told me that means she thought I was her mother. Meanwhile, my actual mother did the bulk of the caretaking: changing Ginger's litter, buying her food, taking her to get groomed. I got to exclusively give and receive affection while doing no work, usually the remit of a grandparent.

Will this pet be allowed outside or be indoors only?

Ginger was allowed outside because none of us were militant enough at the border. She vanished for hours, exploring the woods just beyond our backyard: hiding, hunting, probably loving on some second, secret family. Each night before bed, I did my one duty: called her back inside with a series of unique little *tisk-tisks* and *bbbbbrowws*. Instantly, Ginger appeared from the trees and galloped across the yard into my arms. On the rare night she didn't come (playing a card game with her other, certainly less interesting family), she'd appear the next morning by the door, cold or bored, depending on the weather, with a dead bird. Another sign of love, someone told me.

When my parents moved to Myrtle Beach and I to Chicago, Ginger moved indoors. Her days of hunting and visiting her second family were over. I saw Ginger less often when I moved away and watched from afar via photos as she aged. There was enough distance between us that I didn't cry when she died.

"In your brother's arms on the way to the vet," Mom told me. "He buried her outside his window, put a little stone to mark it."

If applying for particular cats, have you read their descriptions in full, paying special attention to any medical needs?

When a married couple asked me to house-sit what looked like a mansion, I said yes. When they said, "Help yourself to wine," I decided to take a bottle from their cellar every visit. When they let me know they had two dogs, I discovered the catch.

John and I effectively moved into their home during these sits. Our first kiss was in the California king in one of their guest bedrooms; we cooked in a kitchen bigger than either of our apartments and watched movies on a TV that rivaled IMAX. But there were the dogs.

Dog-sitting wasn't too difficult at first: twice-daily feeding and some medications. Someone else came to walk them every day, but I was ultimately responsible for their well-being while their owners were away in Mykonos, the Galápagos, or another island ending in *-os*. At the end of the week, I had to make the unpleasant rounds in the backyard to scoop up all the dogs' poop from the week. If you've ever heard a dog owner discuss the consistency of their dog's shit with the precision of a scholar, it's because there is a fundamental difference between cleaning up a turd that is firm and mopping one up that is pancake batter.

As the dogs aged, my canine responsibilities increased. Soon, my charge included the lovely task of helping one of the pups poop by inserting a thermometer into his ass. Eventually, I decided no paycheck, amount of house wine, or access to IMAX was worth watching the dogs suffer. When the couple asked me to house-sit again, I said I was busy. When I declined the next offer, they took the hint. When the dogs passed away, they texted me and I sent my love.

If you are adopting with a partner, who will get custody if the relationship ends?

When John and I moved in together, I became a stepmom to Toulouse. Toulouse didn't like being held like Ginger, but he would sit beside you and receive under-the-chin rubs on occasion. John and Toulouse were each other's favorites. Occasionally, I got jealous that John loved the cat more than me, a claim he couldn't deny. On rare, cold nights, Toulouse joined us both in bed, and John and I were delighted to have the extra company.

"Baby Toulouse is in the bed!" he would squeal.

It was my ideal pet scenario once again: still free to give and receive love, but not ultimately responsible for the animal.

When John and I broke up, I said goodbye to Toulouse. I haven't had a pet or boyfriend since.

Are there any circumstances which might entail a dramatic change in your living situation—such as a move across the country or abroad?

I have a dream of suddenly and abruptly moving to Paris. I doubt I ever will, but it's nice to only resent myself for not doing it.

Do you have screens on ALL windows?

I didn't plan on visualizing a cat I haven't adopted falling from the third floor of my tiny studio apartment, frankly, but thank you for that image.

Do you have a plan in place for your cat should it outlive you?

Adopting a cat was supposed to be a balm to my depression; this application seems hell-bent on contributing to it.

Why do you want to adopt a cat or kittens?

The cat would be the first living creature I've had inside my studio.

When I moved into my own place, I thought it might become a fuck palace, but it's become something closer to a monk's chamber. Welcoming someone into my home (four- or two-legged) makes me pre-think how sad I'll be when they leave—for the night, for forever. "'Tis better to have loved and lost than never to have loved at all," goes the poem. I guess you can't have pleasure without pain. A cat nibbling on your chin hurts and feels nice at the same time.

"Are you interested in any other cats?" an email asked a week later. It turned out that Tinkerbell had already been adopted. It could have been a small speed bump in my adoption process, but it was enough to bring me to a stop. The mouse is the only thing I'm trying to say goodbye to.

A SIT-DOWN WITH SATAN

When I scored an interview with the Dark Lord of the Universe, I did a deep dive into his work. I'd grown up on his hits—famine, destruction, mass violence—but to revisit them as an adult lent a certain perspective. This demon once had it all, tried to lead a coup in Heaven, and then was disgraced; in some ways, Satan was the first being to be canceled.

I emailed his publicist and offered to commute to the Underworld and meet him in his Palatial Palace of Despair. Satan declined and opted for somewhere more humble and closer to my apartment in Brooklyn's Park Slope.

We met at the 7th Avenue Donuts and Diner.

"You feel that?" Satan asked.

"What?"

"The humidity."

We sat for a moment before I realized.

"Was that *you*?"

"Came up with it several centuries ago—makes even sunny days insufferable."

Satan ordered an egg salad sandwich with a side salad.

"You don't like fries?"

"Quite the opposite. I love them too much."

Satan was humble, eager to share all he'd learned and not take credit for anything he hadn't. It turned out that climate change was humans, though he had the idea at the same time (parallel thinking).

"So much is automated now, I barely go into the office. Humans have really taken a lot of initiative and cause plenty of suffering without my intervention."

"Do you miss it? The hands-on torture?"

"Sometimes."

He swam a piece of lettuce through his ranch dressing like steering a canoe through the river Styx.

"How are you and Jesus?"

He locked eyes with his publicist, seated two tables over. She started to stand, but he, with only his eyes (and perhaps demon-tongue power) kept her seated.

"We haven't really spoken since the breakup. I wish him nothing but the worst."

"Why did it end?"

Another glance to the publicist.

"Honestly? We're too similar."

I changed the topic, not wanting to betray the fast familiarity he'd offered me.

Satan paid our bill and tipped 15 percent.

"Do you play chess?" I asked as we passed a new game store down on Fifth Avenue.

"How about checkers?" he responded.

He turned into the store and asked the clerk for a table. He took red; I didn't question him. We played for a while, swapping some early pieces, as I thought about what it must be like to be where he is in his career. Then, unprompted, he offered an answer.

"I've been working on something pretty big for a while, a legacy project really," he told me.

"What can you say about it?"

"It's a custom torture device." He moved his piece. "King me."

I kinged him.

"It analyzes your life, everything that ever happened, and creates a perfect form of torture that's suited only to you."

"What's mine?" I asked without thinking.

His face sank.

"Why would you want to know?"

"I'm just kidding. Well, I mean, just curious."

"Do you have a guess?" he asked with a grin.

"Maybe moving back in with my parents?"

"That would be the worst thing?"

"I suppose not. Maybe having my heart broken repeatedly? Solitary confinement?"

"If you really want to know . . ."

I nodded. He put down the checker piece in his hand.

"Everything you've been through was part of it. Your parents, your ex, your jobs, your friends, every hell you've been through, and every hell you've created in your mind."

"But I found the meaning in all of that," I countered. "I learned the lesson. I grew."

Satan smiled and jumped my last piece.

"That's the torture, Zach. Making you search for meaning where there is none."

He stood and walked toward the exit, his publicist just behind.

"It was a pleasure talking with you today. Give my best to your parents."

The facade he'd taken on faded as the door closed. I caught a glimpse of his true appearance. He looked like David Duchovny.

BREADSTICKS

It's impossible for me to assess Olive Garden objectively due to the central role it played in my childhood. Thanks to a 20 percent discount at Red Lobster's sister restaurant, the OG was the site of every childhood birthday and graduation celebration. I know what pasta substitutions are allowed and can sing the celebration song "Buona Festa" from memory. The restaurant has such an important place in the sacred lore of my family that on a recent, particularly turbulent flight, I ended what I thought would be my final text to them with "OG Forever."

"I love you unconditionally," my mother told me between bites of a breadstick. I'd taken her out for one-on-one time on a recent Christmas visit home. We played gin rummy, went to the mall together, and made time for a nostalgic pasta date.

"But I can't change what I believe."

"Well, can I bring a boyfriend home to meet you?" I asked between bites of my own breadstick.

"We'll have to cross that bridge when we get there."

I'd just been dumped, so my question was exceptionally hypothetical. Since everything was going fairly well, I decided to ruin it.

"Will you be at my wedding?"

"Zachary."

"It's just a question."

"Well."

She must have felt her love was on trial. I've never questioned that she loves me; it's just how that love manifests and the specific words and actions that accompany it that are up for negotiation. It's a compromise that first flared up in college and culminated at a speech I gave at graduation. I shared a copy of the speech with her the night before I was set to give it to thirty thousand people.

When I got into Princeton, my mom warned me it was a liberalizing, heathenizing institution. But I haven't changed at all. I arrived here a conservative, Southern Baptist carnivore, and tomorrow I'll graduate a gay vegetarian atheist.

"So, you're gay?" Mom asked.

"I thought you knew."

One of two things is supposed to happen when you come out to your parents: (1) They kick you out of their house and send you to conversion therapy to pray the gay away, or (2) they get rainbow tattoos on their forehead, join the Queer Student-Parent Alliance, drive you and your boyfriend, Simon, to prom, and attend every Pride Parade in a hundred-mile radius. Instead, I got:

"Can we not make this the discussion of the weekend?"

It wasn't a clear "Yass!" or "No." It was a "Not right now."

The next day, when I gave my speech, I changed it to "~~gay~~ feminist vegetarian atheist."

Our entrées arrived (Chicken Alfredo and Garlic Herb Chicken con Broccoli with no Garlic Herb Chicken), and I pushed harder.

"Some parents go to Pride Parades with their kids. There are these signs that say, 'I Love My Gay Child.'"

"Is that what you want?" she asked.

I wasn't sure if I did. In fact, my politics have evolved such that I don't go to Pride Parades anymore. But part of me wanted some spectacular act of love, some waterfall of affection to counter the fire-and-brimstone sermons I'd been burned by as a kid.

"You want me to carry an 'I Love My Gay Child' sign in a Pride Parade? I will."

I wasn't sure if she meant it, but it was a surprise from a woman who preached "Homosexuality is a sin" before I knew what homosexuality was.

"Do y'all need anything else?" the server asked with his finger on the bill.

"Should we get the cake?" my mom asked.

Yes, I said with my eyes.

"We'll take one of your celebration cakes," she said.

"Are y'all celebrating anything?"

"No, we just like it," she confessed and laughed.

The server returned shortly with the cake but didn't recruit his coworkers to sing. We ate half and asked for a to-go box to take the leftovers home to Dad.

Mom said we weren't celebrating, but I think we were.

SOME QUESTIONS FOR GOD

- How many people on Earth have a "That's what she said" tattoo?

- How many souls can comfortably fit in Heaven?

- Which founder of a world religion would win in a street basketball tournament? On *Jeopardy*? In the Colosseum?

- Why did my selfie on Saturday, June 14, 2014, receive only fifteen likes?

- Right now, are more people smoking a cigarette, drinking whiskey, or struggling with their relationship with their father?

- Why didn't you answer me?

- How many times is the word *fuck* said each day?

- Am I doomed/destined to become my father? My mother? Maybe both?

- What is the appropriate amount of money to spend on a wedding gift for a couple you don't really like?

- Fuck, marry, kill: Adam, Eve, Satan?

- Will my tweets ever appear in a court of law?

- If you know everything, why do it?

- Do cats have existential angst? Can I be a cat?

- Is Flavortown a city or a county?

- How similar are the Garden of Eden and the Olive Garden?

- When a guy from Grindr likes a years-old photo of you fellating the Eiffel Tower, which base is that?

- How do you figure out who you are in an impossible matrix of inherited identities? Is identity a thing we construct or that we uncover? Is who I am a skyscraper I build or a treasure I find by digging a hole to the center of the Earth? Maybe both?

ACKNOWLEDGMENTS

I'm very grateful to the people who've given of their finite time on this Earth to cultivate, counter, support, engage, and wrestle with the unique collection of experiences and genetics that have given rise to my particular consciousness. tldr: I love you.

The following played a nonzero role in the development of this collection:

Dunkin' Donuts' cold brew, Patty Zimmerman's sense of humor/chaos (her Venmo is Patricia-Zimmerman-7 if you want to send her a tip), Frank Zimmerman's sense of humor/melancholy, their union, which led to my conception, the rest of my family, Chenoa Estrada's guidance, Robert Guinsler's sass, Rob Massar's intelligence, my brilliant editor Becca Hunt's meat cleaver, Halcyon Person's unconditional love, Kyle Turner's "lols" and "LOLs," Jay Jurden's phone calls, Laura Hankin's phone calls, Kate Siegel's texts, The Old Gang's wedding nights, Princeton's endowment for need-based aid, Brooklyn Writers Space's enforcement of quiet in the quiet room, Blythe Roberson's sending of the elevator down (her Venmo is @Blythe-Roberson), my incredible public school teachers, the editors, readers, and literary folk who engaged with and encouraged my work, which include but are not limited to: Emma Allen, Michael Agger, and the wonderful people at *The New Yorker*, Maria Bustillos,

Bobby Hankinson, Stacy Testa, Conrad Person, Tyler Spicer, and Sonya Isenberg; the people and places who've supported my stand-up comedy, which include but are not limited to: Matty Kelly and Andrew Mumm at Union Hall and the Bell House, Jon Boremayo at Stand Up NY, Estee Adoram, Noam Dworman and Liz Furiati at the Comedy Cellar, Robert and Carol Walport and Dec Munro, Daniel Valencia, David Odyssey, Delia Barth, and *Time Out New York*; my Chicago comedy origins (The Second City, iO, The Annoyance), and the comedy scene in New York, David Jopp's love, Doug Scherer's gentleness, Jacob Perlin's selfless support, Chloe Ifshin's encouragement, Seamus Murphy-Mitchell, Hannah K.S. Cantar, the belly laughs of Andy Ward, Martin Scheeler, and Jacob Kosior, John's home-making, the fine people in the city of Paris, and the fine people that run the Olive Garden. To all the twinks I've known and loved, the team at Epicenter, and the wonderful people at Chronicle Books, thank you.

And thank YOU! You read a book. In this day and age, that's cause for celebration.

Buona Festa! *C'est la vie.*